CAREERS

IN SOCIAL AND
REHABILITATION SERVICES

CAREERS
IN SOCIAL AND REHABILITATION SERVICES

GERALDINE O. GARNER

SECOND EDITION

VGM Career Books

Chicago   New York   San Francisco   Lisbon   London   Madrid   Mexico City
Milan   New Delhi   San Juan   Seoul   Singapore   Sydney   Toronto

Library of Congress Cataloging-in-Publication Data

Garner, Geraldine O.
    Careers in social and rehabilitation services / Geraldine Garner.—2nd ed.
        p.   cm. — (VGM professional careers series)
        ISBN 0-658-01058-1 — ISBN 0-658-01060-3 (pbk.)
    1. Social service—Vocational guidance—United States.   2. Rehabilitation—Vocational
guidance—United States.   3. Hospitals—Rehabilitation services—Vocational
guidance—United States.   I. Title.   II. Series

    HV10.5 .G39   2001
    361'.0023'73—dc21   00-68598

VGM Career Books

A Division of The **McGraw·Hill** *Companies*

1 2 3 4 5 6 7 8 9 0   HPC/HPC   0 9 8 7 6 5 4 3 2 1

ISBN 0-658-01058-1 (hardcover)
ISBN 0-658-01060-3 (paperback)

This book was set in Times Roman
Printed and bound by Hamilton Printing

Cover photograph copyright © PhotoDiscs

McGraw-Hill books are available at special quantity discounts to use as premiums and sales
promotions, or for use in corporate training programs. For more information, please write to the
Director of Special Sales, Professional Publishing, McGraw-Hill, Two Penn Plaza, New York,
NY 10121-2298. Or contact your local bookstore.

This book is printed on acid-free paper.

DEDICATION

This book is dedicated to Ms. Lois Cohen, a dedicated social worker who constantly demonstrates her belief in the dignity of each human being with a remarkable sense of calm and humor, and to the memory of her husband, Dr. Jerome B. Cohen, a distinguished scientist and engineer who expected, encouraged, and supported the best of everyone with whom he lived and worked.

CONTENTS

ABOUT THE AUTHOR

Geraldine O. Garner is currently an associate dean and associate professor in the McCormick School of Engineering and Applied Science at Northwestern University. Prior to coming to Northwestern, she taught graduate and undergraduate courses in career development in the rehabilitation counseling department of Virginia Commonwealth University.

Dr. Garner received her B.A. and M.Ed. from The College of William and Mary, and her Ed.D. in career counseling from Virginia Tech. She is the author of a variety of books, articles, and papers, and has received numerous honors for her work in career counseling and career development.

CAREERS

IN SOCIAL AND
REHABILITATION SERVICES

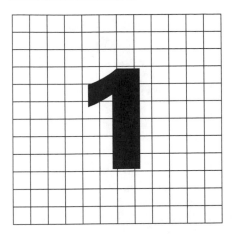

REHABILITATION SERVICES

High-tech advances are all around us. We read about them and marvel at them every day. They are changing our lives in many ways. As a result, one might think that the only career opportunities of the future are those of computer scientist, programmer, or engineer.

That is definitely not the case. As technical advances change the way we live, the work we do, and the health care we receive, human needs and conditions also change. These changes will require increased numbers of workers at all levels.

Professionals in the fields of social and rehabilitation services play a critical role in a multitude of areas including:

- Assisting and advocating for patient access to quality services within the health-care industry

- Helping people with physical, mental, or emotional disabilities to improve their quality of life

- Working with people with substance abuse problems and other addictions

- Working with adult and/or juvenile public offenders

- Working with students in elementary, middle, and high schools as well as colleges and universities

- Serving clients and their families who rely on local, state, and federal government agencies or in military-related organizations

- Collaborating with community organizations and the community at large to attain a higher quality of life for the citizens of the area

- Improving cultural, ethnic, and racial empathy to advance and sustain individual and community growth and development

- Assisting in the promotion of spiritual, ethical, religious, and other human values essential to full development

- Helping to develop healthy family systems

- Counseling in employment and/or career development settings

The professionals in rehabilitation services are those on the front lines of these and other social issues of our time. As a result, careers in the diverse field of rehabilitation services are among the most competitive of all professions.

While helping others is the hallmark of this career field, it is not enough simply to like people. It is important to *really* enjoy working with people and to gain and maintain the knowledge and expertise to do so effectively. Working with people can be exciting and rewarding. It can also be highly stressful and demanding. Therefore, rehabilitation services professionals and social workers must have objectivity, patience, maturity, and appropriate training, supervision, and experience.

THE HISTORY OF REHABILITATION SERVICES

Although social consciousness and concern for others have been part of humanity from the beginning of time, it is widely considered that the 1889 founding of Hull House in Chicago was the birth of the field we now call social work. Hull House represented Jane Addams's philosophy of helping others gain a better standard of living. That philosophy continues today.

After World War I, fields such as social work, occupational therapy, and rehabilitation counseling began to be viewed as true occupations. The turning point was the passage of legislation directed at assisting veterans returning from the war. The legislation of the 1920s forged a relationship between the federal and state governments to provide rehabilitation programs. These programs were initially limited to job retraining and training of veterans. Over time the scope and influence of rehabilitation services professionals and programs have increased.

During the 1930s the social consequences of the Great Depression became the impetus for federal, state, and local governments to work with the private sector to meet the overall needs of all people, not just veterans. But again the emphasis was on jobs.

Subsequent federal legislation in the area of rehabilitation allowed for corrective surgery, therapeutic treatment, and hospitalization. This legislation greatly expanded opportunities in the field and made training and counseling more effective.

When legislation was passed to provide money to train doctors, nurses, rehabilitation counselors, physical therapists, occupational therapists, social workers, and other professionals, the range of professional opportunities in the field of rehabilitation services was greatly expanded. The passage of the Americans with Disabilities Act has had the same impact on the field. More recently, legislation on Welfare to Work has changed the demand for professionals working with the most financially disadvantaged in our society. It has also required the development of new skills in preparing, placing, and supporting clients in their search for employment opportunities, with the goal of lifting these clients out of poverty.

WHAT IS REHABILITATION SERVICE TODAY?

A new age and attitude in rehabilitation services is upon us. It offers a constellation of diverse career opportunities. Each occupation provides a high degree of responsibility and challenge in caring for the special needs of a wide variety of patients and clients. Typically the people served by rehabilitation professionals have personal, social, vocational, physical, educational, and/or spiritual problems.

The Types of Work Performed

Rehabilitation services professionals perform a wide range of duties. The types of responsibilities they perform tend to fall into four categories.

CLIENT SUPPORT RESPONSIBILITIES

Conducting intake

Facilitating logistics and transportation

Motivating clients to continue with their treatment programs

Working with families and significant others

Performing client evaluation and follow-up

TREATMENT RESPONSIBILITIES

Performing crisis intervention

Participating in the development of treatment plans

Coordinating the implementation of the treatment plan

Identifying treatment gaps and overlaps

Conducting individual and group counseling sessions

Providing consultation on special cases

OUTREACH RESPONSIBILITIES

Performing community outreach

Identifying, mobilizing, and coordinating community resources

Seeking and using support networks

Referring clients to other professionals and/or services

Providing education and prevention strategies

ADMINISTRATIVE RESPONSIBILITIES

Reporting and record keeping

Assisting in program development

Training other staff

Providing program consultation

Because the responsibilities of rehabilitation services professionals are closely tied to the health and well-being of other human beings, the levels of authority vary greatly depending on the amount of education and the years of experience one possesses.

Aides perform basic tasks such as personal care and feeding of patients or transportation of clients. This frees the professional and medical staff to concentrate on treatment and therapies. While aides may have a high school diploma, it is generally not required. Consequently, sometimes aides are volunteers who want to see what the field is all about. Some aides are workers who have a real interest in the occupational area but, for various reasons, have not been able to complete the levels of education required for other positions in the field.

Assistants perform support tasks such as patient/client intake and follow-up, treatment setup, and patient assistance. These individuals may or may not have a college degree, but they usually have completed some form of specialized training. This may be on-the-job training, technical school training, or completion of a junior or community college program. In some cases, the preparation may actually be a specialized bachelor's degree program.

Counselors and social workers perform tasks such as facilitating individual and group counseling sessions, administering and interpreting aptitude and interest tests, and making referrals to other professionals. Counselors and social workers have generally completed a master's degree. Some hold doctorates. It should be noted that some people may only have a bachelor of social work (B.S.W.) or bachelor of rehabilitation services. In these instances, the level of responsibility is greatly limited when compared to those of a master's level professional. Counselors and social workers may also be certified by an appropriate professional agency and licensed by the state in which they work.

Therapists generally have completed a related bachelor's and master's degree and additional clinical experience. Some may hold doctorates. They perform specialized treatments designed to rehabilitate patients physically and/or psychologically. Therapists are almost always certified by an appropriate professional group. Some may also be licensed.

Physicians perform medical treatments. The treatments can range from clinical diagnosis to surgery. These professionals have not only completed undergraduate and medical school, they have also participated in an internship and a residency program in their area of specialization. Doctors are licensed and board certified in their clinical area.

Settings in Which Work Is Performed

People in rehabilitation services work in a wide variety of settings. A partial list of the work settings for rehabilitation services professionals includes hospitals; rehabilitation centers; mental health clinics; guidance centers; nonprofit services agencies; federal, state, county, and municipal government agencies; halfway houses and group homes; public and private schools, colleges, and universities; churches and synagogues; correctional institutions and courts; and business and industry. The options are almost limitless.

Characteristics of People in Rehabilitation Services

It is important for those who work in rehabilitation services to care about the needs and welfare of people. While professionals in this area are often characterized as being patient, sincere, and interested in helping others, they also have to be tough-minded in a constructive manner and be interested in effecting positive change. This is not always easy.

Professionals in rehabilitation services should be able to gain the trust of others easily and to think logically. They must communicate well with people, particularly people under a great deal of stress. Their written and oral communication skills should be excellent. Rehabilitation services professionals often have to motivate their clients as well as influence people who can assist and support their clients.

How to Prepare for a Career in Rehabilitation Services

During high school. During high school, it is advisable to take courses in English, a foreign language, mathematics, social science, physical education, and the sciences. In addition to these courses, it is highly recommended that future professionals take elective courses in such areas as government, media, minority studies/literature, psychology, sociology, and anatomy.

High school students who are interested in careers in rehabilitation services should become actively involved in social service clubs and volunteer in their community. Team sports, student government leadership roles, and part-time jobs in social service–related organizations are also highly recommended. The more a high school student works with different populations and in different settings, the easier it will be to focus future studies and experience and develop a sufficient level of expertise to make a significant contribution to his or her chosen field.

During college. Many people major in rehabilitation services, social work, sociology, or psychology to prepare for a career in rehabilitation services. Those planning to enter the field as physicians will need a college curriculum in the physical or life sciences to gain entry to medical school.

A wide variety of majors are good preparation for this field. The liberal arts, the life and physical sciences, the arts, the social sciences, premedicine, engineering, and agriculture all provide an excellent foundation for a career in rehabilitation services.

As in high school, it is extremely important to continue to gain as much related experience as possible. Campus volunteer programs, summer and part-time jobs, academic internships, and cooperative education all provide excellent opportunities to build on the academic foundation of college.

Remember that advancement in this field requires not only higher levels of education but also relevant experience. Therefore, a wide variety of experience during an undergraduate program is extremely helpful in continuing to sharpen one's career focus for employment or graduate/professional school. In some rehabilitation services fields, a graduate degree or medical degree is the minimum education requirement for entry into the field. This is particularly true in many medical fields.

Licensure and certification. There are numerous professions within the rehabilitation field that require licensure or certification. The purpose of licensure or certification is to ensure that all members of the profession meet minimum educational and experience requirements and are competent to practice. In health-care situations, practicing without a required license is usually a serious crime.

Each state establishes its own licensure requirements. Typically, professional licenses are valid only within the state in which they are granted.

There can be significant variations among states regarding the scope of nursing practice and the licensure of psychologists and social workers. However, there can be cases where one state will accept a license issued by another state. This situation, known as reciprocity, permits the professional to move to another state to work without having to take that state's licensure examination.

Some professions require more than one license. In these situations, the additional license or certification is required for a specialty in the particular profession.

What Does the Future Hold?

According to recent commercial and government publications, rehabilitation services occupations are expected to grow faster than average. Predictions gauge that growth will be particularly strong in care for the aging, the homeless, and the mentally impaired and the developmentally disabled.

The growing elderly population will need more adult day care. New methods of treating the mentally and physically disabled will require more group homes and residential-care facilities. Likewise, the number of community-based programs and group residences for the homeless are expected to increase.

What Can I Earn?

Historically, rehabilitation services professions have not typically paid high salaries. To a certain extent this holds true today. However, recently the National Association of Colleges and Employers (NACE) has reported that almost all college-level graduates have been reaping the benefits of a good labor market through higher starting salaries and a greater variety of jobs.

Substantial salary increases have been reported for graduates majoring in liberal arts areas. These are the areas of study that many people pursue before entering the rehabilitation services field. In recent times, salaries have risen between 5.8 and 14.1 percent, with jobs in criminal justice areas among those receiving higher starting salaries. This fact has a correlate in recent government spending in the area of criminal justice and rehabilitation. Close ties have always existed between government funding and social service providers. Salaries in this field tend to indicate the condition of federal, state, and local budgets, which are the source of salaries for many positions in this field.

Generally speaking, high levels of compensation are not associated with most of the occupations in this area. Therefore, it is important not to set earnings expectations too high.

There are areas of rehabilitation services that command higher-than-average salaries. Psychiatry is a good example. However, it is important to note that the areas of rehabilitation services that command higher salaries also require backgrounds that include higher levels of education and often years of supervised clinical experience.

ABOUT THIS BOOK

This book contains an overview of the profession plus chapters on specific occupations within the field of rehabilitation services. Each occupational field is discussed in terms of the work performed, the types of people served, the variety of work settings, the training and qualifications required, and advancement possibilities.

The book also discusses why it is so important that prospective rehabilitation services professionals begin to identify the populations and settings in which they are most interested in working. To help in this process this book will address the different types of people that can be served; the different levels of education necessary for entry into specific occupations; and the wide variety of settings in which to work. These distinctions are very important to career satisfaction and success.

Other chapters in the book discuss (1) career paths and upward mobility in rehabilitation services; (2) professional licensing and certification in the professions; and (3) the impact of technology and legislation on the field of rehabilitation services. The appendixes include lists of professional organizations, licensure and certification organizations, and other resources helpful to the reader.

SO YOU'RE GOOD WITH PEOPLE

One of the chief characteristics of people in the field of rehabilitation services is that they are *good with people*. When rehabilitation professionals are asked why they decided to go into rehabilitation services, they will almost always give this reason.

Being good with people is important in this field. It is a characteristic that each prospective professional needs to examine more closely. It is important that each individual know what being good with people means to him or her. That is the only way to find the right occupational fit within the rehabilitation services field.

HOW TO KNOW WHAT TYPES OF PEOPLE YOU WOULD SERVE BEST

There are many types of people who need the services of rehabilitation professionals. But every rehabilitation services professional cannot be trained in or interested in dealing with *all* of these people. Likewise, there are many types of problems that people have to face, and no rehabilitation services professional is qualified to deal with *all* of them.

When considering a career in social work or rehabilitation services, it is important that the individual consider *what type of people* he or she is most interested in working with and *what type of problems* he or she is most interested in addressing.

Keep in mind that no one is good with all people. And that's OK, because it is important to select a population that will provide the most personal fulfillment in serving. That is what career decision making is all about.

It is important to think about the types of people who need the services of a rehabilitation professional. In preparing for the field of rehabilitation services, each person will want to pursue the type of education that focuses on the group or groups with whom he or she plans to work. This is a necessary first step in the preparation process because rehabilitation services professionals need to become increasingly more knowledgeable about the psychological, sociological, and physiological needs of the population they intend to serve. The following is a collection of comparative questions to start the thinking process.

- *Am I more interested in working with babies than with school children?*
  Yes   No   Neither

- *Am I more interested in working with small children than with teenagers?*
  Yes   No   Neither

- *Am I more interested in working with teenagers than with college students?*
  Yes   No   Neither

- *Am I more interested in working with adults than with children?*
  Yes   No   Neither

- *Am I more interested in working with the elderly than with children or adults?*
  Yes   No   Neither

- *Am I more interested in working with girls than with boys?*
  Yes   No   Neither

- *Am I more interested in working with women than with men?*
  Yes   No   Neither

- *Am I more interested in working with a particular ethnic group or nationality?*
  Yes   No

- *Am I more interested in working with a certain religious group?*
  Yes   No

Likewise, career satisfaction is closely related to higher levels of knowledge about issues that a professional addresses. Therefore, it is important for prospective rehabilitation services professionals to consider the types of human problems that interest them and that they would like to help people address. The range of human problems is extensive, and some people may feel they want to address them all. Fortunately, undergraduate preparation for the field of rehabilitation services provides a broad overview of human problems and conditions. Nonetheless, individuals need to begin to narrow their areas of interest so that they can focus their knowledge and their expertise.

The following is a partial list of issues that rehabilitation services professionals address. The right-hand column allows indication of a high level of interest (HI), moderate level of interest (MI), low level of interest (LI), or no interest (NI).

Homelessness or inadequate housing	HI	MI	LI	NI
Unemployment	HI	MI	LI	NI
Lack of job skills	HI	MI	LI	NI
Financial mismanagement	HI	MI	LI	NI
Illness	HI	MI	LI	NI
Physical disability	HI	MI	LI	NI
Mental disability	HI	MI	LI	NI
Unwanted pregnancy	HI	MI	LI	NI
Teenage pregnancy	HI	MI	LI	NI
Alcohol abuse	HI	MI	LI	NI
Drug abuse	HI	MI	LI	NI
Antisocial behavior	HI	MI	LI	NI
Child abuse	HI	MI	LI	NI
Spouse abuse	HI	MI	LI	NI
Divorce	HI	MI	LI	NI
Family conflict	HI	MI	LI	NI
Criminal insanity	HI	MI	LI	NI

The list can certainly be expanded.

WORK SETTINGS THAT PERMIT YOU TO SUCCEED

Social work and rehabilitation services occupations provide a wide range of opportunities for people to pursue careers in settings that complement their interests and knowledge. These professionals are found in such diverse institutions as:

- Schools
- Hospitals
- Rehab centers
- Correctional institutions
- Business and industry
- Social service agencies—both public and private
- Churches
- Public welfare offices
- Child welfare organizations
- Nursing homes

- Group homes

- Halfway houses

- Consulting services

- Private practices

- Government agencies

Those interested in working in the field of rehabilitation services should begin to identify the settings where they have the most interest and where they have, or are willing to develop, the expertise necessary to serve the specific population.

Using the list on this page and the additional information from the work settings section in each chapter, it is advisable to identify either the areas of interest or areas that can be crossed off the list because of a lack of interest. By so doing, it is possible to narrow the focus and concentrate efforts in preparing for and succeeding in a professional area that meets personal needs, interests, and abilities. This is important in the field of rehabilitation services because success means a positive impact on the quality of life of the people served.

HOW FAR DO YOU PLAN TO GO WITH YOUR EDUCATION IN THE FIELD OF REHABILITATION SERVICES?

As in so many fields, there is a strong relationship between education and advancement. The more education a rehabilitation services professional has, the more opportunities for advancement there will be. However, unlike some professions, there are opportunities for people without high school diplomas as well as for those with advanced and professional degrees in areas such as medicine and law.

The field provides great flexibility for movement, growth, and challenge. Therefore, it is important to think about personal goals when considering the level of education to be completed. To assist in this planning, each occupational description in this book provides information on the level of education needed. The requirements and demands of each field must be balanced against the personal values, abilities, needs, and resources of each prospective professional.

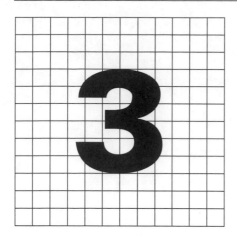

REHABILITATION COUNSELING

Today there are more than 25,000 rehabilitation counselors in the United States. They are playing an important role in the lives of people with disabilities. By working diligently to improve the quality of life for their clients, rehabilitation counselors provide support, training, and opportunities.

The demand for these professionals is expected to grow as societal conditions change. These conditions include homelessness, teenage pregnancies, or the family stress of long-term unemployment. Likewise, advances in medical technology are resulting in more and more lives being saved. The recovery process from illnesses and injuries requires rehabilitation counselors to work with doctors and therapists to help the patient adjust and adapt to the changes that may occur in his or her life. In addition, as the population ages, there will also be a new demand to assure the quality of life that the elderly expect despite diminished capacity. These and other societal changes are expected to increase the demand for rehabilitation counselors by the year 2005.

THE NATURE OF THE WORK

The duties of a rehabilitation counselor vary depending upon the population with whom the counselor works and the setting in which the work takes place. Regardless of the population or setting, rehabilitation counselors help people deal with the personal, social, physical, and vocational impact of their disabilities. They do this by using a combination of techniques such as the following:

- Vocational assessment

- Individual, group, and family counseling

- Medical services coordination

- Vocational services coordination

- Avocational services coordination

- Rehabilitation plan development

- Transferable skills assessment

- Job and task analysis

- Job-seeking skills training

- Labor market surveys

- Job development

- Job placement

By interviewing their clients (and sometimes their families) and by studying medical records and life histories, rehabilitation counselors arrange a program of medical care, vocational training, and/or job placement that meets the clients' needs. They may develop these programs alone or in consultation with other members of a treatment team.

Some rehabilitation counselors specialize in providing personal and vocational counseling for certain types of individuals and/or groups. Others work with a medical team to develop and implement a plan of recovery for patients who have suffered an injury or illness. Still other rehabilitation counselors work with clients to increase their capacity to live and work independently.

In general, rehabilitation counselors evaluate the overall strengths and limitations of their clients to help them find new avenues for meeting their needs, interests, and capabilities. Experienced rehabilitation counselors may become involved in developing and implementing agency programs to address the ongoing and changing needs of their special clients. Examples of this may be the introduction of job training and job-seeking skills for recovering addicts; programs in stress and financial management for the unemployed; and educational programs about community resources for residents of independent living centers.

The populations with whom rehabilitation counselors work vary greatly. Most rehabilitation counselors work only with groups where they have an in-depth knowledge of the clients' abilities, needs, and interests. Some of these special groups include the blind, the mentally ill, the physically disabled, the developmentally disabled, the hearing impaired, the mentally retarded, battered women, autistic children, substance abusers, the elderly, or prisoners.

The clients of a rehabilitation counselor can be of any age, gender, ethnicity, or religion. Again, some counselors specialize within a larger group. For example, a rehabilitation counselor may work exclusively in the area of vocational rehabilitation and only work with veterans of the armed forces.

Some rehabilitation counselors serve not only their clients/patients but also the families of their clients/patients. Often rehabilitation counselors work with other social service professionals, medical specialists, therapists, and prospective employers. The opportunity to interact with people can be very broad in this occupation.

THE SETTINGS IN WHICH REHABILITATION COUNSELORS WORK

Most rehabilitation counselors work for public agencies such as rehab centers, sheltered workshops, nonprofit service agencies, hospitals, special schools, and training institutions. Some work in business and industry, particularly as part of a human resources team. Some work for insurance companies.

Increasingly, rehabilitation counselors are becoming certified and licensed. These professionals usually enter private practice either alone or as part of a group.

TRAINING AND OTHER QUALIFICATIONS

More and more, employers require a master's degree in rehabilitation counseling, counseling and guidance, or counseling psychology. Typically, graduate programs in rehabilitation counseling require course work in five major areas.

1. **Foundations of rehabilitation.** This may include principles of rehabilitation; rehabilitation counseling ethics; the history, philosophy, and legislation of rehabilitation; and disabling conditions.

2. **Client assessment.** This may include client information; principles, types, and techniques of assessments; the interpretation of assessment results; and resources for assessment.

3. **Planning and service delivery.** This may include the synthesis of client information, rehabilitation plan development, service delivery systems and community resources, and case management.

4. **Counseling and interviewing.** This may include theories and techniques in vocational and effective counseling, foundations of interviewing, principles of human behavior, and behavior change modalities.

5. **Job development and placement.** This may include occupational and labor market information; job development; job-seeking skills training, placement, and follow-up.

There are still some employers who will hire those who have only a bachelor's degree in an area such as rehabilitation services or other related fields. In these instances, the responsibilities of the position will probably be limited to the support responsibilities described in Chapter 1.

Employers also may require that rehabilitation counselors be certified by the Commission on Rehabilitation Counselor Certification. Completion of the graduate courses outlined above should be adequate preparation for the certification examination. However, it is highly recommended that the commission be contacted for more in-depth information on the certification process, particularly in specialty areas.

For those who wish to enter private practice, it will probably be necessary to meet the licensing requirements of the state in which practice is planned. Again, it is advisable to contact the appropriate state board of professional licensing to determine the course requirements and the level and amount of experience needed to take the written and/or oral licensing exam. In some states it is necessary to gain additional supervised experience after passing the written examination and before full licensure is granted.

ADVANCEMENT POSSIBILITIES

With increased levels of education and increased years of experience, rehabilitation counselors can be promoted to supervisory positions. In this capacity, they would supervise the caseload of other counselors. They can also be promoted to administrative positions within the agency. This generally moves the rehabilitation counselor out of the area of providing services directly to the client/patient and into the area of program planning and development.

Many times rehabilitation counselors will move to larger agencies in the position of supervisor or director. These moves may or may not include providing direct services to clients/patients.

Those who obtain a doctorate in rehabilitation counseling or a related area may teach and conduct research at the college or university level. As mentioned earlier, others go into private practice alone or as a member of a more comprehensive group of practitioners.

ADDITIONAL SOURCES OF INFORMATION

American Counseling Association
5999 Stevenson Avenue
Alexandria, VA 22304
http://www.counseling.org

American Rehabilitation Counseling Association
5999 Stevenson Avenue
Alexandria, VA 22304
http://www.nchrtm.okstate.edu/arca

Commission on Rehabilitation Counselor Certification
1835 Rohlwing Road, Suite E
Rolling Meadows, IL 60008

Commission on Rehabilitation Counselor Education
1835 Rohlwing Road, Suite E
Rolling Meadows, IL 60008
http://www.core-rehab.org

National Association of Rehabilitation Facilities
P.O. Drawer 17675
Washington, DC 20041

National Council of Rehabilitation Education
c/o Dr. John Benshoff
Rehabilitation Institute
Rehn Hall 317
Southern Illinois University
Carbondale, IL 62901-4609
Website maintained at http://www.nchrtm.okstate.edu/ncre/ncre.html

National Rehabilitation Association
633 South Washington Street
Alexandria, VA 22314
http://www.nationalrehab.org

National Rehabilitation Counseling Association
8807 Sudley Road, Suite 102
Manassas, VA 22110-4719
http://www.nrca-net.org

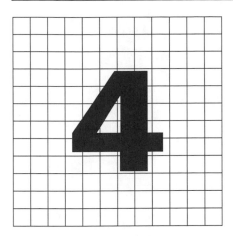

SOCIAL WORK

The field of social work actually came into being before the field of rehabilitation counseling. Social work dates back to the establishment of Hull House in Chicago in the late 1880s. Jane Addams's purpose in founding Hull House was to improve the quality of life for people suffering from poverty, illness, and other life crises. Today, more than 100 years later, social work continues to represent the principles set forth by Jane Addams.

More than 400,000 social workers contribute to the improved welfare of a wide variety of people in the United States. It is a popular notion that social workers are all caseworkers in cities and municipal governments. While the majority do work in the area of public assistance, there are many other settings in which social workers contribute their expertise and their concern for humanity.

THE NATURE OF THE WORK

Social workers help people cope with diverse problems, from antisocial behavior to financial management. Through direct counseling and coordination of services, social workers help clients identify and consider solutions to problems such as homelessness, unemployment, lack of job skills, illness, handicaps, substance abuse, pregnancy, family conflicts, and abuse and neglect. The responsibility for coordinating services for clients is a hallmark of the social work profession.

While there is some overlap, the responsibilities of social workers can be grouped into three categories.

Casework

In this category the social worker is primarily involved in one-on-one counseling with the client. Some examples would include:

- Helping a client deal with an abusive situation
- Identifying needed medical care, education and training, and homemaking services for a client
- Helping a client adjust to a traumatic injury or illness
- Counseling a patient's family

Group Work

In this category the social worker is primarily involved in counseling and working with groups of people. Some examples would include:

- Conducting job-seeking strategies for workers who have been laid off
- Teaching courses in child care for teenage parents
- Working with street gangs to prevent crime
- Conducting group counseling sessions for cancer patients
- Helping groups of people with the same issues find resolution

Community Organization Work

In this category the social worker is primarily involved in outreach to other community organizations in an attempt to identify resources and support for clients served by the agency. Some examples would include:

- Working with child advocacy groups to find foster homes
- Identifying resources to assist families victimized by floods, tornadoes, hurricanes, and other natural disasters
- Coordinating funds and services from the government to serve a local need
- Working in conjunction with the juvenile court

THE PEOPLE WITH WHOM SOCIAL WORKERS WORK

The profession of social work addresses the human needs of all members of society. Individual social workers usually specialize in the types of people with whom they wish to work. There are at least nine specializations in the field of social work.

Child Welfare or Family Services	These social workers assist parents and guardians in identifying services to improve the quality of life for children and families. They may also investigate cases of reported abuse and neglect.
Mental Health	These social workers become involved in such things as crisis intervention, outreach, and individual and group counseling.
Medical	These social workers are members of the medical team composed of doctors, nurses, and therapists that develops treatment plans to help patients cope with chronic or terminal illness and injury. Some social workers specialize within this group as well. They may focus on the needs of transplant, heart attack, cancer, AIDS, or Alzheimer's patients.
School	These social workers help parents, teachers, and students cope with the special problems of children in elementary, middle, or high school. The issues can range from cases of suspected abuse to arranging for other social services to improve the overall quality of life so that the children can get the most from their education.
Community	These social workers become involved in many aspects of a local community including public welfare, housing, and the criminal justice system. Many social workers in this area work with the victims of poverty to assist them in identifying community resources for which they are eligible. Others work with the court system to provide services to juvenile offenders and prison inmates. Some become involved in pre-sentencing investigations of convicted criminals, and some become involved in the investigations of custody suits.
Clinical	These social workers participate in the treatment of patients under the care of psychiatrists and psychologists in mental health institutions. Chapter 6 provides more detailed information about this particular area of social work.
Industry	These social workers are usually members of the human resources departments of business and industry in an effort to address such issues as improved productivity, worker safety, employee turnover, and chronic absenteeism.
Gerontological Services	These social workers are part of a new and emerging field of social work. As the population ages, there is an increasing need to assist the elderly in obtaining appropriate medical, social, and recreational services.

THE SETTINGS IN WHICH SOCIAL WORKERS WORK

State, county, and municipal agencies employ many social workers. These agencies are devoted to such diverse issues as social services, child welfare, mental health, physical health, housing, public welfare, education, human resources, and corrections.

Other social workers are employed in nonprofit social service organizations as well as community and religious programs. Hospitals, rehab centers, recreation programs, nursing homes, and home health agencies also hire social workers. Some social workers become licensed and enter private practice in their community.

TRAINING AND OTHER QUALIFICATIONS

Like rehabilitation counselors, most social workers have a master's degree in social work.

A bachelor's degree in social work, rehabilitation services, sociology, psychology, or another social science is good preparation for the master's degree in social work (M.S.W.). Graduate courses in social work include human growth and development, social welfare policies, and methods of social work. The M.S.W. requires at least one year of clinical experience in an agency, hospital, or school under the direct supervision of an experienced M.S.W.

After two years of supervised experience social workers are eligible for membership in the Academy of Certified Social Workers.

ADVANCEMENT POSSIBILITIES

Like rehabilitation counselors, social workers are able to advance to supervisory positions. Those with the proper education and experience can be promoted to supervisor of caseworkers or director of an agency. It is also possible to move from a small agency to a larger one and assume more responsibility.

As in the case of rehabilitation counselors, an increasing number of social workers are becoming certified and licensed. Many of them establish a private practice alone or with a larger group of professionals.

ADDITIONAL SOURCES OF INFORMATION

American Federation of State, County, and Municipal Employees
1625 L Street NW
Washington, DC 20036
http://www.afscme.org

Council on Social Work Education
1725 Duke Street, Suite 500
Alexandria, VA 22314
(Publishes the *Directory of Accredited B.S.W. and M.S.W. Programs*)
http://www.cswe.org

National Association of Social Workers
750 First Street NE, Suite 700
Washington, DC 20002-4241
http://www.naswdc.org

EMPLOYMENT SERVICES

Work activities that are valued by society and that give an individual a feeling of purpose are as important to people with disabilities as they are to abled individuals. Therefore, rehabilitation services professionals who work in the area of employment services strive to provide employment and training opportunities to a wide variety of people in a wide variety of circumstances.

It has long been recognized that a person's self-concept is primarily defined by the work that he or she performs. If people are asked to describe themselves, they are likely to begin their description by saying that they are a lawyer, a teacher, an engineer, a programmer, a banker, and so on. Therefore, when disabling conditions such as developmental disabilities or illness or injury prevent a person from pursuing an occupation, it can be both financially and psychologically devastating.

The trauma of not being able to continue in one's job or profession has been found to have profound consequences on psychological well-being. Many studies have shown that the loss of a job is almost as traumatic as the death of a spouse or a child. Consequently, many professionals in rehabilitation services work with people who have vocational and employment problems.

People who suffer unexpected physical and mental disabilities may need to change their occupations. They have an obvious need for the vocational knowledge and expertise of trained rehabilitation professionals. Likewise, special populations such as teenage mothers, drug addicts, dislocated homemakers, or laid-off workers also need the services of professionals trained in vocational/career testing, goal setting, job search, decision making, and/or placement.

There are many occupations related to employment services in the field of rehabilitation services, and the future demand for these professionals looks very good. The rapidly changing nature of the workplace and recent legislation, which opened opportunities for people with disabilities, mean that there will be a continuing need for professionals who can assist special populations in entering the workforce in new numbers.

In addition, the workplace of the future will demand a new level of technologically related skills. Therefore, business and industry will look to professionals in the area of employment services to substantiate the skill level of each applicant.

VOCATIONAL EVALUATOR

The Nature of the Work   Vocational evaluators measure and assess the vocational interests, knowledge, and skills of individuals seeking to perform certain jobs. The individuals served by vocational evaluators may include physically and mentally disabled clients as well as healthy ones. It is important that vocational evaluators be knowledgeable about the reliability of interest, aptitude, and achievement tests related to specific jobs.

These professionals measure and evaluate skills in a wide variety of job areas. They may test a person's ability in such areas as keyboard knowledge, computer software and hardware knowledge, mathematical and analytical ability, and industrial and technological expertise. They may also evaluate an individual's ability to use certain types of office or industrial equipment. They also test a person's interest in specific occupational areas.

Some vocational evaluators may be responsible for placing their clients in work settings and monitoring their progress. In these positions, vocational evaluators work closely with local businesses and industries. Some vocational evaluators work together with other professionals to serve as advocates for these clients. The advocates may include such people as teachers, counselors, therapists, and doctors.

The People with Whom Vocational Evaluators Work   As stated earlier, the primary group of people served by vocational evaluators includes physically and mentally disabled clients. They may also include groups such as laid-off or unemployed workers, high school dropouts, teenage mothers, workers injured on the job, and displaced homemakers.

Vocational evaluators also interact with other professionals. They often confer with lawyers, insurance companies, employers, and other career counselors.

The Settings in Which Vocational Evaluators Work   Vocational evaluators work in a wide variety of settings. Some of these settings are rehabilitation centers, public and private schools, community colleges, trade schools, community agencies, employment centers and private businesses, and labor unions.

Some vocational evaluators are self-employed. They maintain private practices to evaluate individuals for specialized training programs or specific jobs.

Training and Other Qualifications

A college degree is generally required. Many positions require a master's degree in a counseling-related area. Some vocational evaluators must be licensed by the state in which they work. In these cases, it may be necessary to have graduated from an accredited graduate program.

Course work in test and measurement is highly desirable. An in-depth knowledge of testing methods and test interpretation is an important job requirement today. The legal responsibilities of vocational evaluators make their work extremely important to both their clients and their employer.

Each state has its own licensing requirements for vocational evaluators to become self-employed. Individuals interested in this career opportunity should confer with the state board for licensing and certification of professionals.

Advancement Possibilities

There are many opportunities for vocational evaluators to advance in their careers. Because of the quantitative nature of their expertise, vocational evaluators are in demand.

Experienced vocational evaluators can assume supervisory positions in large agencies. In these settings, the vocational evaluator has responsibility for a team of evaluators. Other vocational evaluators who have gained increasing amounts of experience and who have pursued higher levels of education can move into counseling, therapeutic, or administrative positions. Experience and education greatly expand the vocational evaluator's opportunities for advancement.

VOCATIONAL REHABILITATION COUNSELOR

The Nature of the Work

The sudden loss of the ability to perform a job due to an accident or an illness can be very traumatic. Vocational rehabilitation counselors help people deal with the impact of disabilities on their jobs and careers. Vocational rehabilitation counselors not only work with individuals who have suddenly suffered a loss of ability, but they also work with people who have congenital and developmental disabilities.

After conferring with their clients, vocational rehabilitation counselors develop and implement educational and support programs to increase their clients' employability. They help their clients make wise vocational decisions. Therefore, they must have a good understanding of their clients' potential as well as the skills that are in demand and the training programs available to prepare them for the job market.

The People with Whom Vocational Rehabilitation Counselors Work

Vocational rehabilitation counselors work with individuals who are old enough to enter the workforce. Consequently, they do not work with young children. The clients of vocational rehabilitation counselors have physical, mental, and/or emotional barriers that can inhibit their full participation in a job or career.

Some counselors specialize in serving a particular type of client. For example, some may work with the blind or the hearing impaired. In these areas, counselors may do as much work with employers as with the client. They may help the employer adapt the work environment to accommodate a hearing- or sight-impaired employee. Likewise, they will work with the client to prepare him or her for the expectations of the workplace.

Other vocational rehabilitation counselors may work with the mentally or emotionally disabled or clients who have suffered the loss of their capacity to continue in a career field because of injury or illness. In these instances, the counselor may need to interact with others such as occupational therapists, special education teachers, and the client's family.

The Settings in Which Vocational Rehabilitation Counselors Work

Vocational rehabilitation counselors work in job training and vocational rehabilitation centers, state employment offices, veterans' programs, and colleges and universities. They also work in private and government-sponsored social service programs. While some vocational rehabilitation counselors are self-employed as private practice counselors, most work in agencies that provide free vocational counseling and job placement to disabled clients.

Training and Other Qualifications

A master's degree in rehabilitation counseling is generally a minimum requirement. However, a master's degree in other counseling areas may be acceptable. These areas include, but are not limited to, counseling and guidance, mental health counseling, or counseling psychology in which course work in career counseling, individual appraisal, and occupational information was completed. In some small agencies and communities, people with a bachelor's degree in rehabilitation services, counseling services, psychology, or other related fields may be acceptable to work with vocational rehabilitation clients.

Advancement Possibilities

The more experience vocational rehabilitation counselors gain in vocational testing, career and employment counseling, and job development, the more opportunities they will have for advancement. Likewise, increased levels of education will qualify vocational rehabilitation counselors for supervisory and administrative positions within their current organizations or larger agencies.

Vocational rehabilitation counselors who aspire to administrative positions sometimes find it helpful to take graduate courses in public administration or business administration. These courses enhance their ability to prepare and defend agency budgets and to monitor the impact of federal, state, and local legislation and regulations on the agency and its clients.

CAREER COUNSELOR

The Nature of the Work

Career counselors assist a wide range of people in making career decisions related to entering the workforce, reentering the workforce, or making a career change. While vocational rehabilitation counselors specialize in assisting persons with disabilities in making career decisions, career counselors generally work with a wider range of individuals who are faced with making career decisions.

Career counselors assist their clients in exploring and evaluating their education, specialized training, work history, career and personal interests, job skills, personal strengths and weaknesses, and physical capacities. To do this, career counselors often conduct or arrange for aptitude, achievement, and/or interest testing. They also spend a considerable amount of time working with their clients individually or in groups to help each person become more aware of his or her own potential, set more realistic career goals, and develop a plan of action to accomplish the goals.

In addition to counseling, career counselors can also become involved in teaching job-seeking individuals resume writing and job interviewing skills. They may also assist clients in applying and competing for jobs that match their preparation, skills, and interests.

The People with Whom Career Counselors Work

Career counselors work with a wide range of people involved in making career and/or life decisions. The groups with whom career counselors work can range from elementary students who are becoming aware of the wide variety of career options through their schoolwork to laid-off workers who must now find new jobs or change career fields.

In some instances the clients of career counselors are not under pressure to make career decisions. However, most of the time career counselors are working with clients who are under a great deal of pressure. They may be college or high school students who must find a first job but who have not really thought through personal interests, strengths, needs, and goals. Or they may be displaced homemakers or widows who suddenly find that they need to enter or reenter the workforce but feel they have no marketable skills.

Career counselors often specialize in working with certain types of groups who are making career decisions. However, unlike other occupations within employment services, career counselors can be generalists. Their knowledge of tests and measurement, vocational development stages, theories of decision making, occupational information, and the job market makes it easy for them to adapt to different groups of people over the course of their careers.

The Settings in Which Career Counselors Work

Many career counselors work in public and private high schools and colleges. Career counselors are also employed in job training and vocational rehabilitation centers. Some community agencies and special programs employ career counselors to assist individuals who are affected by corporate downsizing and other shifts in the job market.

In recent years, some career counselors have been employed by government agencies, business organizations, and major industries to assist in retraining, promoting, and outplacing employees. Others have entered private practice to provide these services. Career counselors in private practice must meet appropriate licensing requirements in their states.

Training and Other Qualifications

The minimum requirement for a career counseling position is a master's degree in a counseling-related discipline. The areas of study most appropriate for career counseling positions are career counseling, counselor education, guidance and counseling, college student affairs, school counseling, rehabilitation counseling, and counseling psychology.

Graduation from a program accredited by the Council for Accreditation of Counseling and Related Educational Programs or the Council on Rehabilitation Education may be an important consideration for those planning to become certified or licensed. Because each state differs in its requirements, it is important to contact the appropriate board for licensure or certification.

Advancement Possibilities

Advancement in career counseling can differ from other types of counseling because of the wide variety of settings in which career counseling can be carried out. For example, career counselors who are employed in public school systems can become directors of guidance for their school or supervisors of guidance for their school district or state.

Career counselors employed in colleges and universities can become directors of career planning and placement centers. Some career counselors in higher education and in industry have been promoted to the position of vice president for student affairs in colleges or vice president of human resources in business and industry.

Those who obtain a doctorate can become counselor educators and teach or do research in colleges and universities. Others may pass state licensing requirements and go into private practice. Still others may develop a consulting practice serving educational and employment organizations.

SUPPORTED EMPLOYMENT COORDINATOR

The Nature of the Work

Supported employment has become the newest method of providing employment and training opportunities for persons with severe disabilities. In the past, sheltered workshops provided the only opportunities that these individuals had for learning job-related skills.

Sheltered workshops were operated by institutions where adolescents and adults with severe disabilities lived. They did not provide an opportunity for these adolescents and adults to experience some of the rewards of the regular workplace.

Today the emphasis is on providing supported employment environments for people with severe disabilities. This can mean training and supervising clients in paid jobs in regular work settings or operating commercial enterprises in the community. Within these commercial enterprises, small groups of clients provide a service or do assembly work that has been contracted with local businesses.

There are four models for supported employment.

1. **Supported job model.** This program places adults and adolescents in regular jobs in the community and provides training and support. At each work site, there is a job coach for each worker. The job coach teaches the person how to perform the job.

2. **Enclave model.** This program places a small group of people (five to six) with severe to moderate disabilities in regular assembly jobs in business and industry to work with normal workers. A job coach and a trained employee of the business or industry are present to teach the members of the group how to do the job.

3. **Mobile crew model.** This program is so named because the community agency establishes a business to provide services to local business and industry under contract. Small groups of disabled workers are taken to each job site to perform such functions as groundskeeping and janitorial services.

4. **Benchwork.** The community agency operates a small, single-purpose nonprofit corporation, which performs a function under contract to individuals and/or businesses. Examples of this type of work may be stripping furniture or routine assembly work.

It is the supported employment coordinator's responsibility to identify and analyze these types of jobs and businesses to determine their suitability for the special population to be served.

The clients in supported employment need intensive, ongoing supervision and training to do each job. In small programs, the supported employment coordinator may also provide the individual training and supervision at the job site. In larger programs, that function is performed by the mental retardation job coach.

The People with Whom Supported Employment Coordinators Work

Supported employment coordinators work with a diverse group of people. In addition to working with severely to moderately retarded adults and adolescents, they also work with public officials and with business men and women in the community.

To support participating employers as well as individuals with severe disabilities, supported employment coordinators interact with other social service professionals to identify needed resources in the community.

The Settings in Which Supported Employment Coordinators Work

While a few supported employment coordinators are employed by industry, the majority are employed by nonprofit community agencies. These agencies get most of their funding from federal and state government.

In addition to spending time in the agency, much of the supported employment coordinator's time is spent in business and industry. It is there that the supported employment counselor either develops job opportunities or trains and supervises clients.

Training and Other Qualifications

Small nonprofit agencies may accept applications from people with a bachelor's degree in rehabilitation services, counseling services, psychology, or another related field. However, some positions may require a master's degree in a counseling-related area.

Advancement Possibilities

The more experience supported employment coordinators gain, the more opportunities they have for advancement. Likewise, increasing levels of education qualify them for supervisory and higher-level administrative positions within their current organizations or in larger agencies.

Supported employment coordinators who aspire to administrative positions sometimes find it helpful to take graduate course work in public administration or business administration. This preparation enhances their ability to prepare and defend agency budgets and to monitor the impact of federal, state, and local legislation and regulations on their agency and clients. Courses in business administration give supported employment counselors a better understanding of the needs and demands of the businesses and industries with which they work.

MENTAL RETARDATION JOB COACH

The Nature of the Work

Mental retardation job coaches, otherwise known as MR job coaches, are important members of the supported employment program. They motivate and prepare severely to moderately mentally retarded clients to work in jobs outside of the residential institution. The MR job coach works with each employer to identify all of the steps in a job and carefully designs an individually tailored training process to teach the job to a client.

In most cases the MR job coach learns the job and performs the job for the employer for a brief time before bringing the client to the work site. When the special worker arrives at the job, the MR job coach is there until it is certain that the individual can perform the job without constant supervision. This process can take weeks or months depending on the individual and the severity of the disability.

The MR job coach returns on a regular basis to check on the individual and his or her job performance. The caseload for most MR job coaches is only four to six individuals because of the time-consuming nature of the training and supervision.

The People with Whom Mental Retardation Job Coaches Work

MR job coaches generally work with severely to moderately retarded adults and adolescents. Occasionally, they also work with people with severe physical disabilities. They also work closely with employers and their regular employees. It is important that the MR job coach identify a model worker from among the regular employees. This individual works closely with the MR job coach to train the client and to learn about the capabilities and limitations of the individual's disability. When the MR job coach no longer comes regularly, the model worker assumes the supervision of the special worker on a day-to-day basis.

The Settings in Which Mental Retardation Job Coaches Work

MR job coaches are employed by nonprofit community agencies that serve severely to moderately disabled individuals. However, most of their time is spent in the community on regular job sites. Their clients may only work three to six hours per day, but the preparation time requires that the MR job coach spend much more time than that at the work sites.

In general, service industries tend to be the primary employers in supported employment programs. Therefore, the MR job coach is likely to be working in restaurants, hotels, and offices.

Training and Other Qualifications

A college degree is generally required. A bachelor's degree in rehabilitation services, social work, sociology, psychology, special education, or a related field would be considered the most appropriate preparation.

Advancement Possibilities

There are opportunities for MR job coaches to become supported employment coordinators or supervisors of other MR job coaches. They may go to a larger community agency where responsibilities will increase. Like almost every occupation in this category, the more education and experience a person has, the more opportunities he or she will have for advancement.

ADDITIONAL SOURCES OF INFORMATION

American Counseling Association
5999 Stevenson Avenue
Alexandria, VA 22304
http://www.counseling.org

Association for Career and Technical Education
(formerly American Vocational Association)
1410 King Street
Alexandria, VA 22314
http://www.acteonline.org

Career Planning and Adult Development Network
541 Cowper Street
Palo Alto, CA 94301
http://www.careernetwork.org

Commission on Rehabilitation Counselor Certification
1835 Rohlwing Road, Suite E
Rolling Meadows, IL 60008

Council for Accreditation of Counseling and Related Educational Programs
American Association for Counseling and Development
5999 Stevenson Avenue
Alexandria, VA 22304
http://www.counseling.org/cacrep

National Board for Certified Counselors
3 Terrace Way, Suite D
Greensboro, NC 27403
http://www.nbcc.org

National Career Development Association
5999 Stevenson Avenue
Alexandria, VA 22304
http://www.ncda.org

National Employment Counseling Association
(a division of ACA)
5999 Stevenson Avenue
Alexandria, VA 22304
Website maintained at http://www.geocities.com/Athens/Acropolis/6491/
    neca.html

MENTAL HEALTH SERVICES

At times everyone is confronted by personal, professional, and social problems. Often these problems seem insurmountable. Therefore, it is not surprising that every year more than 30 million people seek the help of mental health professionals.

These professionals use a wide variety of approaches to help their clients and patients deal with issues related to mental and emotional health. They also work in a wide range of settings where their work can be both physically and emotionally demanding. However, all of these professionals have one thing in common—they are committed to promoting optimum mental health for their clients and patients.

PSYCHIATRIC SOCIAL WORKER

The Nature of the Work   The field of social work offers a wide variety of career options. However, one of the most important branches is the field of psychiatric social work. Psychiatric social workers are an integral part of most mental health teams, which are made up of psychiatrists, therapists, nurses, and counselors. They often serve as the liaison between the patients and their families and the psychiatrists or psychologists. In some cases, the psychiatric social worker may also serve as the ombudsman between the hospital and the patient and/or the family when misunderstandings occur.

Psychiatric social workers gather data about the patient and the circumstances in which the patient lives. They prepare family histories and conduct interviews of all parties who play a significant role in the life of the patient. All of this information is vital in planning the overall treatment program.

Some aspects of the treatment program can be provided by the psychiatric social worker. In addition, it is often the psychiatric social worker who explains the treatments and their purpose to the patient and the family. These treatments can include individual, group, and/or family counseling as well as medical intervention.

The People with Whom Psychiatric Social Workers Work

Psychiatric social workers generally work with patients who have been hospitalized with mental or emotional disorders. They may also work with the families of the patients.

Some psychiatric social workers specialize in certain types of mental illness and/or certain types of people with mental and emotional disabilities. For example, a psychiatric social worker may work exclusively with autistic children or with adult schizophrenics or with the criminally insane.

Psychiatric social workers interact professionally with doctors, therapists, nurses, and mental health counselors. Sometimes they are supervised by other psychiatric social workers. However, most often they are directly supervised by psychiatrists or psychologists.

The Settings in Which Psychiatric Social Workers Work

While psychiatric social workers may work for the same agencies and institutions as other social workers, most are employed by state or local mental hospitals or mental health agencies. They may also work in the psychiatric units of general hospitals.

Some psychiatric social workers are employed by nursing homes and other medical facilities. Still others go into private practice. Often this is a group practice with a team of other mental health professionals.

Training and Other Qualifications

Psychiatric social workers must have a master's degree in social work with a specialization in psychiatric social work. This is in addition to the traditional graduate courses in human growth and development, social welfare policies, and methods of social work. This specialization requires a heavy concentration of course work in psychology.

All graduate students in social work are required to do at least one year of clinical experience in an agency, hospital, or school under the direct supervision of an experienced M.S.W. However, psychiatric social work students must complete their clinical experience under the direct supervision of psychiatrists or clinical psychologists.

Like other social workers, the psychiatric social worker is eligible for membership in the Academy of Certified Social Workers after two years of supervised experience. This certification and state license qualify the psychiatric social worker to enter private practice.

Advancement Possibilities

Psychiatric social workers can advance to supervisory positions. Those with the proper education and experience may be promoted to unit supervisors or program directors. It is also possible to move from a small hospital to a larger one and assume more responsibilities. Those who complete a doctorate may teach and conduct research in a university setting. In addition, social workers are often required to be licensed by the state in which they practice. Holding licensure as a social worker provides more opportunities for advancement.

Additional Sources of Information

American Federation of State, County, and Municipal Employees
1625 L Street, NW
Washington, DC 20036
http://www.afscme.org

Council on Social Work Education
1725 Duke Street, Suite 500
Alexandria, VA 22314
(Publishes the *Directory of Accredited B.S.W. and M.S.W. Programs*)
http://www.cswe.org

National Association of Social Workers
750 First Street, NE
Suite 700
Washington, DC 20002-4241
http://www.naswdc.org

MENTAL HEALTH COUNSELOR

The Nature of the Work   Mental health counselors use an array of counseling techniques to treat the mentally disabled. These techniques can include the following:

- Individual counseling

- Group therapy

- Outreach

- Crisis intervention

- Skills training in everyday living

- Social rehabilitation

Like the psychiatric social worker, mental health counselors are usually part of a mental health team. The other members generally include psychiatrists, psychologists, psychiatric nurses, and social workers. It is the goal of this team to restore full mental health to the patient, although this is not always possible.

Frequently mental health counselors specialize. They may concentrate in such areas as addiction and substance abuse, marriage and family problems, suicide, stress management, problems of self-esteem, issues associated with aging, or vocational and educational decisions. As a specialist, the mental health counselor is able to provide more in-depth services to the patient.

The People with Whom Mental Health Counselors Work

As stated earlier, because mental health counselors can work with a wide range of individuals and groups, most specialize. They work with specific groups. As a result, the other professionals with whom mental health counselors interact vary depending on the area of specialization.

For example, mental health counselors who work with public offenders primarily interact with the court system and officials in correctional institutions. Those who specialize in child abuse and neglect interact with family members, social workers, and medical professionals.

The Settings in Which Mental Health Counselors Work

Like psychiatric social workers, most mental health counselors work in public or private mental hospitals or clinics. They may also work in the psychiatric units of comprehensive hospitals or in public and private mental health programs. With proper certification and licensure, some mental health counselors go into private practice. They may work alone or with a group of other mental health professionals.

Training and Other Qualifications

Mental health counselors hold master's degrees in mental health counseling. However, there are some mental health counselors who hold master's degrees in psychology, social work, or a related counseling discipline. Increasingly, hospitals and clinics are requiring a Ph.D. in mental health counseling.

Mental health counselors are certified by the National Academy of Certified Clinical Mental Health Counselors. To become certified, mental health counselors must hold a master's degree and complete a period of supervised clinical experience, submit a taped sample of clinical work, pass a written examination, and complete two years of post-master's experience under the supervision of another certified mental health counselor.

Advancement Possibilities

Mental health counselors often advance to directors or supervisors of counseling in their agencies or hospitals. When this is not possible, mental health counselors may move from a small organization to a larger one.

As in other areas of mental health services, mental health counselors who become certified and licensed in their state can enter private practice. Some who complete doctoral degrees teach and conduct research at colleges and universities.

Additional Sources of Information

National Academy of Certified Clinical Mental Health Counselors
5999 Stevenson Avenue
Alexandria, VA 22304

SUBSTANCE ABUSE COUNSELOR

The Nature of the Work

Substance abuse counselors work with people who are addicted to drugs and/or alcohol. Most substance abuse counselors work as part of a team that may include physicians, psychologists, social workers, and nurses who are dedicated to helping clients/patients overcome addiction to various chemical substances.

While substance abuse counselors are involved with individual and group counseling, they also participate in the evaluation of patients. In cases where pretreatment detoxification is warranted, the counselor refers the patient to an appropriate facility.

Therapy for the patient can include individual, group, and/or family counseling. Counselors in this area confront the patient with facts and information about his or her addiction. Because denial is a part of addiction, it is important that this confrontation be carried out in an instructional manner. Exhibiting a judgmental manner is not only unacceptable, it is counterproductive in the recovery process of addicts.

Many substance abuse counselors have either experienced addiction themselves or they know people who are or have been addicted. This can give substance abuse counselors credibility with patients, particularly as they try to help the patient overcome denial. In these cases, substance abuse counselors use not only their expertise but also their experience with addiction to reach their patients.

The People with Whom Substance Abuse Counselors Work

Unfortunately young people, adults, and the elderly can all be victims of substance abuse. The illness strikes all races and ethnic groups. Therefore, substance abuse counselors generally work with a wide range of people who suffer from the same problem. Some substance abuse counselors decide to specialize and work with particular groups of people. For example, some professionals may work only with teenagers and others only with public offenders.

On a professional level, substance abuse counselors must interact with medical personnel such as doctors, nurses, and therapists. Those who work in business and industry also work with the managers and supervisors of employees who have exhibited substance abuse problems that affect their work.

The Settings in Which Substance Abuse Counselors Work

Generally the treatment programs are specialized. They address either alcohol addiction or drug addiction. Within these specializations, there are usually further subdivisions depending on the characteristics of the client. For example, treatment programs differ for teenagers and for adults. Recently there has been recognition that new and different methods of treating women's addiction must be implemented. Treatment methods can differ for patients who seek help voluntarily or for those who are mandated to be in a treatment program by the courts or their employers.

Substance abuse counselors work in hospitals and in special treatment centers for persons with chemical addictions. Those who have advanced training, certification, and licensure may be in private practice. Sometimes the private practice is with a group of other health professionals who have specialized in the area of substance abuse.

Training and Other Qualifications

In the past, substance abuse counselors have sometimes had little or no formal training. Typically they themselves had overcome addiction or had been close to people with chemical addictions. However, increasingly higher levels of specialized education and training are being required for entry into this field.

Now it is common for substance abuse counselors to have completed the same basic master's program as other counseling or social work professionals. However, they also do course work in the areas of therapy and therapy techniques associated with chemical addiction. Supervised internships are also common in the area of chemical dependency.

Advancement Possibilities

Advancement in substance abuse counseling is not unlike advancement in other areas of counseling and social work. Substance abuse counselors are able to advance to directors or supervisors of counseling either in their agencies or hospitals. In other cases, they may move from small agencies to larger ones.

Those who obtain doctorates can also join the faculty of colleges and universities that teach and do research in the area of substance abuse counseling. Those who become certified and pass state licensing requirements may go into private practice. Others do research and consulting.

Additional Sources of Information

National Clearinghouse on Alcoholism and Drug Abuse Information
P.O. Box 2345
Rockville, MD 20852
http://www.health.org

National Institute on Drug Abuse
6001 Executive Boulevard
Bethesda, MD 20892-9561
http://www.nida.nih.gov

PSYCHOLOGIST

Psychologists treat and observe individuals through testing, counseling, and controlled research experiments. Psychologists can also become involved in teaching and administration.

The Nature of the Work

Psychologists are a very important group within mental health services. Their education and training prepare them to use a systematic approach to understanding and explaining human behavior. By using such methods as interviewing, testing, and observation, psychologists attempt to explain the needs and the behaviors of individuals and groups. As members of a mental health team, psychologists observe and treat the emotional and physical reactions of their patients.

In general, psychologists concentrate in one of the following specializations.

- **Clinical psychology.** This specialization focuses on the direct treatment of patients who have mental and emotional disorders. Clinical psychologists use a wide range of treatment techniques. These can include such things as psychoanalysis, behavior modification, or medication to help patients cope with the issues that confront them. In the United States there are more than 25,000 clinical psychologists.

- **Counseling psychology.** This specialization focuses on normal people who are having difficulty coping with personal conflicts. The counseling psychologist uses some of the same techniques as the clinical psychologist to help clients face their anxieties, emotional difficulties, or interpersonal conflicts.

- **Developmental psychology.** This specialization focuses on the study of behavioral changes that occur at different stages of life. Developmental psychologists attempt to define, measure, and explain different types of behavior that occur from birth to death. Areas such as vocational and emotional development require that the developmental psychologist explain behaviors that almost all humans experience as well as individual differences that occur in the development process. By doing so, the developmental psychologist helps define abnormal changes in development.

- **Social psychology.** This specialization focuses on how humans are affected by the environment in which they live. Social psychologists study the ways in which people interact with one another and with their environment. They may study the influences of the family, school, or work setting on the behavior of individuals.

- **Experimental psychology.** This specialization focuses on scientific experiments on particular aspects of behavior. These studies may be conducted to determine animal or human behavior. The results of these studies can help explain such things as motivation for behavior or steps in the learning process. This is the largest specialization within the field of psychology.

- **Psychometrists.** This specialization focuses on the measurement of intelligence, personality, and aptitude. Psychometrists use a wide array of tests to develop a profile of a client or patient for the clinical or counseling professional. They are knowledgeable in the areas of test construction, test administration, and test interpretation.

- **School psychology.** This specialization focuses on both diagnostic and remedial work with a wide range of special children in the public and private school setting. School psychologists can be involved in diagnosing such things as learning disabilities and gifted and talented students. They work with parents, teachers, and children to facilitate the educational success of children.

- **Educational psychology.** This specialization focuses on the way children and adults learn. Unlike the school psychologist, who may diagnose and treat a learning problem, the educational psychologist studies the learning process from a scholarly perspective.

- **Industrial psychology.** This specialization focuses on the relationship between employees and their work environments. Industrial psychologists study such things as work and motivation, job satisfaction, productivity, and ergonomics. They advise management on changes in the work environment that will improve productivity, morale, and satisfaction.

- **Engineering psychology.** This specialization focuses on the design of engineering systems where people interact with machines. Engineering psychologists not only contribute to increased productivity but also to increased worker safety. Often, engineering psychologists develop teaching aids to help train workers to operate and use new equipment in a safe and effective manner.

The People with Whom Psychologists Work

Like other occupations within the field of rehabilitation services, psychologists who work in the clinical and counseling areas of the profession can work with all types of people. However, clinical and counseling psychologists often specialize in and treat only certain groups of people. For example, some psychologists treat children, while others specialize in treating college students, working adults, women, or the elderly.

Psychologists may also specialize in the types of mental disorders they treat. For example, some may treat people who are suffering from depression. Others may treat manic depressives or schizophrenics. And there are others who specialize in personality disorders, including multiple personalities.

As mentioned earlier, many psychologists teach and do research within a college or university setting. Those who work in an academic setting primarily work with other colleagues and graduate students in conducting their research. Many teach undergraduate and graduate courses. However, the primary group of people with whom these psychologists interact is other professionals. By publishing and speaking about their research findings, this group of psychologists expands the basic knowledge of the field.

The Settings in Which Psychologists Work

While the popular image of the psychologist's workplace is an office where therapy sessions take place, the fact is that most psychologists work in colleges and universities. This is partially attributed to the fact that more than 60 percent of psychologists hold Ph.D.s. Interestingly, more psychologists are involved in teaching and research today than are involved in clinical practice.

Nonetheless, psychologists do work in private clinical practices and in hospital settings. They are employed in public and private mental hospitals as well as in the psychiatric units of comprehensive hospitals. Psychologists are employed in group homes and halfway houses. Some work for government agencies; others do consulting for business and industry.

Training and Other Qualifications

Because the opportunities for people with only a bachelor's or master's degree are quite limited, a doctorate in psychology is highly recommended. For those planning to go on to graduate school in psychology, an undergraduate degree in psychology is excellent preparation. Upon completion of the undergraduate degree, students can be admitted directly into some Ph.D. programs.

Some universities that do a lot of research in the area of psychology may be able to offer an entering Ph.D. student a graduate fellowship or assistantship, which pays for tuition and fees and provides a monthly living stipend while completing doctoral studies. These graduate fellowships and assistantships go to the best students applying for entry into the program. Therefore, it is important to do well in the undergraduate program and gain related experience through internships, practica, or cooperative education.

Completion of a graduate program approved by the American Psychological Association (APA) is important. Many positions, particularly university teaching and counseling positions, require a degree from an APA-accredited institution.

Advancement Possibilities

Advancement within the field of psychology is difficult for those who do not have a graduate degree. Those with a bachelor's degree in psychology can successfully pursue a professional career outside of psychology in an area that requires a good understanding of human nature. An example might be a position in human resources in business and industry. However, within the field of psychology, the opportunities are extremely limited.

This holds true even for those with a master's degree in psychology. The master's degree qualifies a person for assistant positions to Ph.D. psychologists involved in research, administration, or counseling.

Psychologists who hold Ph.D.s and are employed on the faculty of colleges and universities can advance through a system called tenure and promotion. After a certain number of years of teaching and doing research, college and university faculty have their teaching and research reviewed by other faculty in their department, then their school, and then their university. After the review, the faculty member may be given tenure. This means that he or she can continue to do research and teach at that institution for the remainder of his or her professional life. There is also a promotion from assistant professor to associate professor. Later in an academic career, a faculty member can request another review for promotion to full professor—the highest level attainable.

Psychologists who are in the clinical or counseling areas have somewhat the same process of advancement described for rehabilitation counselors and social workers. Those who become certified and licensed can enter private practice. Those who work within hospitals and agencies can advance to supervisory and then administrative positions. They also have the option to move from smaller agencies to larger ones, with increasing amounts of responsibility for caseload and/or management.

Additional Sources of Information

American Association of State Psychology Boards
P.O. Box 4389
Montgomery, AL 36103

American Board of Examiners in Professional
    Psychology
2100 East Broadway, Suite 313
Columbia, MO 65201
http://www.abpp.org

American Board of Professional Psychology
2100 East Broadway, Suite 313
Columbia, MO 65201-6082
http://www.abpp.org

American Board of Rehabilitation Psychology
750 First Street NE, Suite 100
Washington, DC 20002
http://www.apa.org/divisions/div22/ABRP.html

American Psychoanalytic Association
309 East 49th Street
New York, NY 10017
http://www.apsa.org

American Psychological Association
750 First Street NE, Suite 100
Washington, DC 20002
http://www.apa.org

Association of Black Psychologists
P.O. Box 55999
Washington, DC 20040-5999
http://www.abpsi.org

National Association of School Psychologists
4340 East West Highway, Suite 402
Bethesda, MD 20814
http://www.naspweb.org

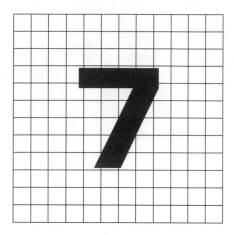

MEDICAL SERVICES

One of the fastest growing segments of our economy is the medical profession. Often it is assumed that this simply means a demand for more doctors and nurses. However, the medical profession offers a broader array of career possibilities than that. In fact, one of the fastest growing areas in the medical field is medical rehabilitation.

There are four trends that are creating an increasing demand for people in rehabilitation services occupations related to medical services.

1. Managed care has become the predominate method whereby people receive medical services. Medical workers, other than doctors, follow cases and determine the level and duration of health care to be provided. Increasingly, health maintenance organizations (HMOs) and other insurance providers employ nurses, therapists, and counselors to form patient health-care teams.

2. The baby boomers are aging. That means a larger percentage of our population will soon be categorized as elderly. They will require more health care. As people experience diminished capacity due to injury, illness, or simply the aging process, there will be a greater need for professionals to help them cope and compensate.

3. New technology is improving the quality of health care. As a result, there is a higher survival rate among those who are sick or injured. This means that these patients will need assistance in recovering from or coping with their medical conditions.

4. There is a new emphasis on preventive care and nutritional services. Our society has become more health-conscious. People seek out fitness and nutrition experts to maintain their physical and mental well-being.

These phenomena combine to create more opportunities and diversity among the career options in rehabilitation services. From traditional psychiatrist to dietitian and nutritionist, the occupations in this group represent the blending of medicine, psychology, science, and technology to improve the quality of life.

PSYCHIATRIST

The Nature of the Work

Psychiatrists must complete all the training required of any medical doctor. After finishing medical school, these professionals not only complete at least a one-year internship, they also complete a four-year residency in psychiatry. In other words, they are trained in both medicine and psychology.

This teaches them the techniques for diagnosing and treating the mental, emotional, and behavioral disorders of patients. Unlike the psychologist, psychiatrists examine patients following standard medical procedures. They first determine the physical condition, including laboratory and other diagnostic tests. Then using a systematic approach to gather the medical and mental histories, they attempt to determine when and how the disorder began. Often family histories become an important part of determining the nature and extent of the mental disorder.

After diagnosing the problem, psychiatrists formulate a treatment plan. This can involve other members of the medical team such as nurses, therapists, social workers, and counselors. It can also involve family members, coworkers, or court-appointed officials.

To treat their patients, psychiatrists use therapies such as psychotherapy, group therapy, and medications. Many times they will use a combination of these therapies.

Psychotherapy is the most widely used technique among psychiatrists. It involves the patient talking to the psychiatrist about his or her problem. During this process the psychiatrist asks the patient to explore feelings and insights in more detail. By helping patients explore their feelings, psychotherapy helps them arrive at a personal understanding of the root cause of their problem. It takes years of training to become proficient in this powerful technique.

The People with Whom Psychiatrists Work

While some psychiatrists teach and do research in medical schools as well as colleges and universities, most work in clinical settings. And like psychologists who work in these settings, psychiatrists work with all types of people who have mental, emotional, and behavioral disorders.

Like psychologists, psychiatrists often specialize and treat only certain types of people or disorders. Psychiatrists may treat such groups and conditions as abused children, emotionally disturbed teenagers, professional people under high stress, trauma victims, and others. They may also specialize in treating mental and emotional disorders or antisocial behavior.

The Settings in Which Psychiatrists Work

Many psychiatrists are in private practice. Sometimes the private practice can include other rehabilitation services professionals such as counselors, social workers, or specialized therapists. To be able to admit their patients, when necessary, psychiatrists in private practice are also affiliated with a hospital.

Some psychiatrists are exclusively staff doctors at either private or public hospitals. A smaller number of psychiatrists work for community or government agencies. Some specialties within psychiatry such as industrial psychiatrists or forensic psychiatrists work in settings such as business and industry or the courts and correctional institutions.

Training and Other Qualifications

In high school, people who plan to go into psychiatry should take a rigorous college preparatory curriculum including English, languages, humanities, social studies, mathematics, biology, chemistry, and physics. In college, the premedical adviser should be contacted to ensure that the appropriate college major and course electives are taken to prepare for entry into medical school.

Typically, college students preparing to go on to medical school major in biology, chemistry, biomedical engineering, or a special major called premed. In some cases students who have majored in a liberal arts or social science area, such as psychology, have gone on to medical school. However, in these cases they have often taken a number of physical and life sciences courses as electives in order to prepare.

It is necessary to take the standardized admissions test for medical school. Most students take the Medical College Admissions Test (MCAT) in their senior year of college. It is an important part of the medical school admission process. After four years of medical school and one year of specialized training, usually in an area such as internal medicine or pediatrics, doctors preparing for the field of psychiatry complete a four-year residency in psychiatry. During the residency, they are paid members of the staff of a psychiatric unit of a teaching hospital.

When considering the nine years of preparation beyond college, it is worthwhile to consider how long it takes to complete the typical Ph.D. degree. In some cases, completion of the M.D., plus the residency, is not significantly longer.

Advancement Possibilities

For psychiatrists in private practice, advancement comes in the form of professional recognition in the field and a sizable practice in an area of specialization. Prestige and status in the community contribute to wider recognition of the accomplishments of these professionals.

For those psychiatrists who practice on the staff of a hospital or agency, the opportunities for advancement are similar to other professionals in the field of rehabilitation services. They can be promoted to supervisory and administrative positions, and they can move to larger hospitals and agencies. Some may be asked to join the teaching faculty of medical schools.

**Additional Sources of
Information**

American Medical Association
535 North Dearborn Street
Chicago, IL 60610
http://www.ama-assn.org

American Psychiatric Association
1400 K Street NW
Washington, DC 20005
http://www.psych.org

Association of American Medical Colleges
2450 N Street, NW
Washington, DC 20037-1126
http://www.aamc.org

National Institute of Mental Health
6001 Executive Boulevard
Bethesda, MD 20892
http://www.nimh.nih.gov

National Mental Health Association
1021 Prince Street
Alexandria, VA 22314-2971
http://www.nmha.org

PROSTHETIST AND ORTHOTIST

Of the thousands of professionals in the field of rehabilitation services, there is one small group of specially trained professionals whose goal it is to improve the quality of life for those who suffer from debilitating conditions and loss of limbs. These are the prosthetists and orthotists. There are fewer than 2,500 of them in the United States, but their work is vitally important to the patients and doctors they serve.

The Nature of the Work Professionals in the areas of prosthetics and orthotics become involved in the design, production, and fitting of devices that assist people with disabilities to simulate normal functions. **Prosthetists** design, make, and fit special devices for patients who have experienced total or partial loss of a limb. The devices they make are referred to as prosthetic devices.

While prosthetics date back to the days of wooden legs, today's prosthetic devices are made of advanced plastics and graphite composites. Gone are the immovable artificial limbs. Advances in this field have led to a number of components, including the foot, the ankle, knee controls, sockets, support systems, and skin-like coverings. In addition, mechanical switches, harnesses, or electric signals control the modern prosthetic device.

These advances in the field give the patient lightweight, durable, aesthetically pleasing replacement limbs. A good prosthetist must be well trained and knowledgeable about the newest developments in the prosthetic field.

Orthotists design and make braces, irons, stays, and splints, otherwise known as orthoses, for patients who suffer from disabling conditions resulting from accidents, disease, or congenital problems. The devices designed by orthotists provide needed support to the affected parts of the body.

Because orthotists treat a wide range of problems, most of their work requires that they custom fit devices for patients. This process includes interaction with the patient to prepare castings or impressions for the orthotic device. As a member of the patient's rehabilitation team, the orthotist continues to follow-up with the patient after the device is fitted.

The People with Whom Prosthetists and Orthotists Work

Prosthetists and orthotists work as part of a rehabilitation team of doctors, nurses, and therapists. Because they are involved in making the devices, these professionals also interact with business and industries that supply the materials and equipment to produce prosthetic and orthotic devices. It is not uncommon for prosthetists and orthotists to collaborate with materials engineers, biomedical engineers, mechanical engineers, or electrical engineers in the design and development of new devices.

Most important, they work directly with patients to present choices about different devices. They also help patients make decisions about the most appropriate design to fit their lifestyle and health condition.

Prosthetists typically work with accident victims and victims of disease, such as diabetes and cancer. They also work with children and the elderly. Generally, the prosthetist first sees a patient approximately six weeks after surgery. At that point, the patient is fitted for a preparatory prosthesis. The permanent prosthesis is usually prepared and fitted several months later, depending on the individual's recovery rate. Periodic checkups help ensure a good fit, so prosthetists develop long-term professional relationships with their patients.

Orthotists' patients include victims of such conditions as cerebral palsy, spina bifida, hemophilia, spinal cord injuries, brain damage, stroke, muscular dystrophy, arthritis, and multiple sclerosis. Orthotists typically work with a qualified technician to make the appropriate device for each patient.

Like the prosthetist, the orthotist is a member of the patient's rehabilitation team. Depending on the condition, the orthotist may develop a long-term professional relationship with some patients. However, because the orthotist also treats victims with minor injuries from accidents or sporting events, the relationship with patients can be short-term as well.

Like so many professionals in the field of rehabilitation services, prosthetists and orthotists often specialize either in certain groups of people or in particular types of disabilities. Specialization limits the people with whom the prosthetist and orthotist work. For example, some may only work with athletes and orthopedic doctors. Others may work exclusively with cancer patients and oncologists. The options are almost limitless.

The Settings in Which Prosthetists and Orthotists Work

Prosthetists and orthotists work in diverse settings. They can be employed by health-care industries involved in the manufacture of prosthetic and orthotic devices. They can also work in privately owned facilities or laboratories. There are more than 1,500 such member companies in the American Orthotic and Prosthetic Association.

Some hospitals and specialized medical facilities also employ prosthetists and orthotists on staff. However, almost all prosthetists and orthotists see patients in the hospital. They often must examine patients after surgery or an accident to begin the process of fitting them for a device. They may also see patients in the hospital again if the device needs to be altered due to changing health conditions.

Training and Other Qualifications

While some people prepare for this field with a bachelor's degree in engineering or science, others obtain an undergraduate degree in prosthetics or orthotics from one of the board-approved programs at colleges and universities in the United States. Those who obtain a degree in another discipline can complete postgraduate course work in prosthetics and/or orthotics. To be certified, a person needs an additional year of clinical experience if his or her undergraduate degree is in prosthetics or orthotics. If the undergraduate degree is in another area, one to two additional years of clinical experience may be required for certification.

This field requires certification by the American Board for Certification in Orthotics and Prosthetics. While the number of certified orthotists is only slightly larger than the number of certified prosthetists, almost one-third of all people certified by the board are certified in both fields.

Continuing education is imperative in this field. It is important to know that prosthetists and orthotists cannot maintain their certification without continued education.

Advancement Possibilities

Certification and increasing amounts of experience assure prosthetists and orthotists that they will be able to advance in their field. Experienced prosthetists and orthotists supervise technicians in industry and laboratories. Like other rehabilitation services professionals, prosthetists and orthotists can move from small facilities and hospitals to larger ones. In these instances they generally take on more supervisory and administrative responsibility.

Additional Sources of Information

American Academy of Orthotists and Prosthetists
1650 King Street, Suite 500
Alexandria, VA 22314
http://www.oandp.org

American Orthotic and Prosthetic Association
1650 King Street, Suite 500
Alexandria, VA 22314
http://www.theaopa.org

National Commission on Orthotics and Prosthetics Education
1650 King Street, Suite 500
Alexandria, VA 22314
http://www.ncope.org

MEDICAL SOCIAL WORKER

The Nature of the Work
Medical social workers are members of a unique group of social workers who specialize in helping patients deal with their medical problems. They are an important part of health teams composed of physicians, nurses, and therapists who develop treatment plans to help patients cope with injury and chronic or terminal illness.

Medical social workers may focus on the needs of transplant, heart attack, cancer, AIDS, or Alzheimer's patients. They gather medical data about the patient and the circumstances in the patient's life that may affect his or her medical condition. Some examples of the types of work that medical social workers might do range from monitoring psychological, as well as physiological, reaction to treatment and medication to assisting a terminally ill patient in preparing a will.

In addition, the medical social worker may serve as the liaison among the doctors, the therapists, the patient, and the family. In fact, it is sometimes the medical social worker who has the responsibility of explaining the treatments and their purpose to the patient and the family. In some cases, the medical social worker, like the psychiatric social worker, serves as an ombudsman between the hospital and the patient and/or the family.

The People with Whom Medical Social Workers Work
Medical social workers generally work with patients in public and private hospitals. Some medical social workers may specialize in working with certain types of illness or certain types of people. For example, a medical social worker may work exclusively with geriatric, hospice, or AIDS patients, or he or she may work with terminally ill children.

In general, medical social workers are members of a team including doctors, therapists, counselors, and nurses. Medical social workers generally work under the direct supervision of doctors.

The Settings in Which Medical Social Workers Work
While some medical social workers may work for the same government and community agencies or institutions as other social workers, most are employed by hospitals, nursing homes, hospice programs, and other medical facilities.

With home health care increasing, some medical social workers go into private practice. Often this is a group practice with a team of other health professionals dedicated to providing outpatient and home health care.

Training and Other Qualifications

Medical social workers must have a master's degree in social work with a specialization in medical social work. These studies include graduate courses in human growth and development, social welfare policies, and methods of social work. This specialization requires a heavy concentration of medically related course work.

All graduate students in social work are required to have at least one year of clinical experience in an agency, hospital, or school under the direct supervision of an experienced M.S.W. However, medical social work students must complete their clinical experience under the direct supervision of experienced medical social workers and doctors.

Like other social workers, medical social workers are eligible for membership in the Academy of Certified Social Workers after two years of supervised experience. Attaining certification and a state license qualifies medical social workers to enter private practice.

Advancement Possibilities

Medical social workers are able to advance to supervisory positions. Those with the proper education and experience can be promoted to unit supervisors or program directors. They move from a small hospital or health-care facility to a larger one and assume more responsibilities. Those who complete a doctorate may decide to teach and conduct research in a university setting.

Additional Sources of Information

American Federation of State, County, and Municipal Employees
1625 L Street, NW
Washington, DC 20036
http://www.afscme.org

Council on Social Work Education
1725 Duke Street, Suite 500
Alexandria, VA 22314
http://www.cswe.org
(Publishes the *Directory of Accredited B.S.W. and M.S.W. Programs*)

National Association of Social Workers
750 First Street, NE
Suite 700
Washington, DC 20002-4241
http://www.naswdc.org

DIETITIAN AND NUTRITIONIST

Today people are much more conscious of their diet. Even fast-food restaurants have begun to provide nutritional information about the foods they serve. While most people tend to think about dietitians and nutritionists in hospital settings, these professionals are playing a more important role in the lives of healthy individuals as well.

The Nature of the Work

Dietitians and nutritionists are responsible for planning meals that are not only high in nutritional value but are also appropriate in content and texture to meet the needs of special populations. In addition, some dietitians and nutritionists purchase food, equipment, and supplies as well as prepare meals. Others may supervise a professional staff that has the responsibility for purchasing and preparing meals.

It is common for dietitians and nutritionists to be counselors and educators as well as food scientists. They instruct and advise individuals and groups in the proper diet to meet specific needs such as reducing calories, fat, cholesterol, and/or carbohydrates in the diet. Special physical or medical conditions can also require reeducation on how to eat. In these cases, the dietitian or nutritionist may prepare printed materials as well as lectures.

There are generally seven areas in which dietitians and nutritionists can specialize.

- **Administrative or management dietitians.** These people oversee the planning and operation of major food service systems. The responsibilities of this specialization include administration of personnel, design and implementation of training programs, planning food systems, and developing departmental budgets.

- **Chief dietitians.** These professionals perform all of the responsibilities of administrative or management dietitians; however, they are usually found in hospital settings and have the added responsibility of clinical management as well as food service management. Specifically, chief dietitians monitor and maintain the records on each patient's dietary needs and reactions.

- **Clinical or therapeutic dietitians.** They plan and supervise the preparation of diets to meet patient needs. In these cases, either the patient's condition or the attending physician requires a special diet as part of the recovery process. Clinical dietitians are part of the medical team and advise patients, families, doctors, medical staff, and hospital administration on patients' dietary needs.

- **Community dietitians.** These specialists counsel individuals and groups on proper nutrition. As a member of community health programs, the purpose of dietitians in this specialization is to maintain health and prevent disease in the local community.

- **Business dietitians.** They perform a wide range of functions for various businesses and industries. Sometimes they appear in the media on behalf of grocery store chains. Often, they will advise consumers on how to shop for nutritional foods that are in season or that fit a tight budget. Many business dietitians work for the food or restaurant industries. They also work on new product development and sales.

- **Education dietitians.** They teach food science and nutrition as well as food service courses in colleges and universities. They may also teach in hospitals. Many write books and publish articles about food and nutrition.

- **Dietitian consultants.** They have private practices where they advise major industries on food science and nutrition issues. Some conduct seminars for other professionals, and still others work under contract with nursing homes, health department programs, and hospitals to provide diet and nutrition counseling to patients and clients. Athletic programs at the collegiate, Olympic, and professional levels also employ dietitians and nutritionists to tailor dietary plans to the fitness needs of athletes.

The People with Whom Dietitians and Nutritionists Work

All types of people need the counseling and guidance of dietitians and nutritionists. While it is common to think of these professionals in hospital settings, the increasing concern for fitness has increased the demand for their expertise. Some of the groups that dietitians and nutritionists serve include schoolchildren, expectant mothers, the elderly, diabetics, heart attack patients, athletes, overweight individuals, people recovering from serious illnesses, and people with severe allergies.

The Settings in Which Dietitians and Nutritionists Work

The largest number of dietitians and nutritionists are employed in public and private hospitals. However, many are also employed in community health programs. They also work in fitness centers, wellness clinics, health maintenance organizations (HMOs), doctor's offices, training camps for athletes, public and private school systems, and business and industry.

Training and Other Qualifications

Dietitians and nutritionists are trained in the science of food and nutrition. An undergraduate degree in foods and nutrition or food service management is a basic requirement for entering this field.

Typically these programs of study include courses in foods and nutrition, food service management, chemistry, bacteriology, physiology, mathematics, psychology, sociology, and economics. In addition, a one-year internship is required.

Advancement Possibilities

As the dietitian or nutritionist gains experience, he or she will often move from salaried positions to private practice. This trend is expected to increase as public agencies downsize their staff and contract for specialized services.

Other dietitians and nutritionists become directors and administrators at schools, hospitals, and health-care or government agencies. Like other rehabilitation services professionals, they sometimes move from small agencies and organizations to larger ones where they take on increasing amounts of responsibility. Those with advanced degrees teach and do research in colleges and universities.

Additional Sources of Information

American Dietetic Association
216 West Jackson Boulevard, Suite 800
Chicago, IL 60606-6995
(312) 899-0040
http://www.eatright.org

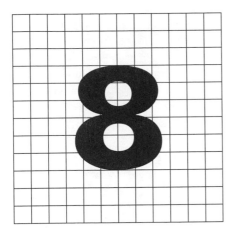

THERAPEUTIC SERVICES

According to the U.S. Department of Labor, the occupations known as therapists are concerned with the treatment and rehabilitation of persons with mental, emotional, and physical disabilities. In their work, therapists develop or restore functions, prevent loss of physical capacities, and maintain optimum performance.

Therapists generally work in medically oriented institutions or programs where the therapy provided is directed at improving the patients' educational, occupational, and/or recreational skills. The strategies of these therapists may include such means as exercise, creative arts, massage, heat, light, water, electricity, and specific therapeutic apparatus. Generally these strategies are prescribed by a physician and implemented by a medically oriented team of professionals that includes not only therapists but also physicians, nurses, social workers, and counselors. Because of the teamwork nature of these professions, all therapists must be exceptionally competent in their record keeping. Every other member of the team relies on the therapist's input for diagnosis and treatment purposes. Therefore, the records must be accurate and up to date.

As a result of the aging of our population and new medical technology that increases the survival rates of critically ill patients and increases the practice of early discharge from hospitals, there is a growing need for all types of therapists. In addition, the enactment of the Americans with Disabilities Act has created a new demand for therapists, particularly occupational therapists, to help businesses and industry meet the requirements of the law.

PHYSICAL THERAPIST

The Nature of the Work Physical therapists are the team members concerned with people who need to regain some or all of their ability to move following disease, injury, or loss of limb. Every physical therapist has three primary goals: to restore function, to relieve pain, and to prevent disability. To accomplish this, physical therapists evaluate, develop treatment plans with the rehabilitation team, and work with each patient.

The approach begins with a thorough review and evaluation of the patient's medical records and proceeds to testing, measuring, and evaluating the patient's overall physical condition. After gathering this data, the physical therapist prepares a treatment program and then plans and administers the therapeutic treatment.

Treatment can include such things as manual therapeutic exercises, application of physical agents, massage, and traction. Therapeutic exercises are generally designed to improve and maintain muscle function. The physical agents that these therapists can use include such things as light, heat, water, and electricity. Examples of these agents are whirlpool baths, moist packs, ultraviolet light, and infrared lamps. Massage and traction are often administered to relieve pain.

Some physical therapists evaluate, fit, and adjust prosthetic and orthotic devices. They may also recommend modifications to the devices to improve usefulness to the patient. In addition to conferring with prosthetists and orthotists, they also confer with physicians and other health practitioners involved in the rehabilitation of their patients.

Physical therapists become involved in instructing, motivating, and assisting patients in exercises and other forms of treatment. They also instruct family members in the physical therapy procedures being used to rehabilitate the patient. They may also be responsible for orienting, instructing, and directing the work activities of physical therapy assistants and aides.

Some may plan and conduct lectures and seminars for medical and professional staff, physical therapy students, and/or community groups. Those with advanced education and experience may train and evaluate clinical students or conduct research and write technical articles and reports for publication.

The People with Whom Physical Therapists Work

Like many rehabilitation services occupations, physical therapy serves all types of people. However, like other professionals, physical therapists often limit treatment to specific patient groups and/or disabilities. Some of these specialties include pediatric physical therapy, pulmonary physical therapy, neurological physical therapy, and geriatric physical therapy.

The Settings in Which Physical Therapists Work

Many physical therapists work in hospitals and rehabilitation centers. However, increasingly, physical therapists are employed in home health agencies, nursing homes, hospices, sports medicine centers, athletic departments of colleges and universities, and fitness programs in business and industry. Some are in private practice either alone or with other professionals such as orthopedic surgeons and oncologists.

Training and Other Qualifications

The basic educational requirement to enter the field of physical therapy is a bachelor's degree in physical therapy. For those who have a degree in another field, a postgraduate certificate in physical therapy is required. After 2002, post-baccalaureate degrees will be required of all new physical therapists. There are currently 173 colleges and universities offering degrees in physical therapy.

The course work required for a degree or certificate in physical therapy includes chemistry, anatomy, physiology, neuroanatomy, biomechanics, human growth and development, manifestations of disease and trauma, evaluation and assessment techniques, research, and therapeutic procedures. Students must also complete a period of supervised clinical experience.

It is important to note that the knowledge needed in this field is expanding rapidly and, therefore, many employers require a master's degree. Admission to these programs is highly competitive. Upon graduation from an accredited physical therapy program, all states require that physical therapists pass a licensure examination.

During high school, the best preparation for a career in physical therapy is a strong background in physical and biological sciences. In addition, it is advisable to do volunteer work in a physical therapy setting.

For those who do not plan to pursue a graduate degree in physical therapy, a career in this area is still possible as a physical therapy assistant. Physical therapy assistants work under the direct supervision of a physical therapist. They carry out treatment plans, train patients in exercises and use of special equipment, and report patient progress. Licensure is not required in all states for physical therapy assistants.

Advancement Possibilities

Experienced physical therapists can become supervisors and directors in the hospitals and clinics in which they work. If they are employed by a small hospital or clinic, they can do what so many professionals in rehabilitation services do—they can move to larger organizations. Sometimes physical therapists move from salaried positions in hospitals to private practice. This trend is expected to increase as many agencies begin to use contract services to provide specialized health-care delivery. Those with advanced degrees often teach and do research in colleges and universities.

Additional Sources of Information

American Physical Therapy Association, Inc.
400 West 15th Street, Suite 805
Austin, TX 78701
http://www.apta.org

OCCUPATIONAL THERAPIST

The Nature of the Work

Occupational therapists are an important part of the medical team that works to help people with mental, physical, developmental, or emotional disabilities relearn day-to-day skills. When this is not possible, occupational therapists help their patients compensate for lost skills due to illness or injury.

By tailoring treatment programs to meet the unique needs of each client, the occupational therapist plays an important part in the development and implementation of an overall treatment plan. Some of the responsibilities of the occupational therapist may include the following:

- Planning manual and creative arts activities for restoration or adaptation of skills

- Practicing prevocational, vocational, and homemaking skills for daily living

- Participating in educational, recreational, and social activities designed to help regain physical or mental functioning or adjust to handicaps

- Designing and constructing special equipment and suggesting adaptations to living arrangements to maximize personal independence

In addition, occupational therapists consult with other members of the medical team including doctors, nurses, and social workers or counselors. They may also conduct training seminars for patients, families, or other professionals. Some make and fit adaptive devices in consultation with prosthetists and orthotists.

The People with Whom Occupational Therapists Work

Occupational therapists almost always work with individuals in special groups or with particular disabilities. According to the American Occupational Therapy Association, occupational therapists significantly improve rehabilitation for many people with impairments due to arthritis, cancer, or other debilitating illnesses; head or spinal cord injuries; orthopedic, work, or sports-related injuries; amputation; burns; head trauma; stroke and other neurological conditions; mental illness; or development disabilities. Some occupational therapists evaluate the abilities and needs of children and recommend treatment and equipment adaptation to maximize their learning in a school environment. Others work with the mentally ill, mentally retarded, or emotionally disturbed. Others work with substance abusers or people with eating disorders. Like so many occupations in rehabilitation services, the specialties within occupational therapy seem almost limitless.

The Settings in Which Occupational Therapists Work

The largest percentage of occupational therapists work in traditional acute, rehabilitative, or psychiatric hospitals. The second-largest percentage work in public school settings, where they assist parents, teachers, and children in adapting and developing functional skills for daily living. Other settings in which occupational therapists work include nursing homes, home health-care agencies, clinics, community mental health agencies, consulting firms, and private practice.

Training and Other Qualifications

Occupational therapists must be certified by the American Occupational Therapy Certification Board. This requires passing the certification examination after completion of a four-year degree from an accredited occupational therapy program or the completion of a postgraduate certificate or master's degree in occupational therapy, when the undergraduate degree is not in occupational therapy.

Course work in occupational therapy programs includes biology, chemistry, physiology, anatomy, neurology, psychology, and sociology. All accredited programs of occupational therapy require at least a six-month clinical internship. However, some will require more than that. In the United States, there are more than 300 accredited programs in occupational therapy at the associate's, bachelor's, and master's levels.

Currently 28 states require licensure in addition to passing the national certification examination. With fewer than 40 graduate programs in occupational therapy, it is becoming increasingly competitive to enter this field.

Advancement Possibilities

Occupational therapists generally begin their careers as staff therapists, and after several years of experience they gain the status of senior therapist. Senior therapists may become involved in supervising occupational therapy students and volunteers in addition to assuming more administrative responsibilities. People with master's degrees can move into teaching, research, and program director positions.

Additional Sources of Information

American Occupational Therapy Association
4720 Montgomery Lane
P.O. Box 31220
Bethesda, MD 20824-1220
http://www.aota.org

ART THERAPIST

The Nature of the Work

Art therapists are unique members of a patient's rehabilitation team. After conferring with other members of the team to determine the nature of a patient's illness, the art therapist recommends a treatment plan and conducts programs to instruct the patient in art techniques. Both psychological knowledge and creative art skills are used.

Appraising the patient's various artistic statements can be an important part of the patient's recovery process. The progress and regression of each patient are reported to other members of the treatment team so that adjustments and adaptations can be made in the overall treatment plan.

According to the American Art Therapy Association, art therapy is an effective treatment for developmentally, medically, educationally, socially, or psychologically impaired persons.

The People with Whom Art Therapists Work

Most art therapists work with individuals. They also work with families and groups. Like other rehabilitation services professionals, they may specialize in terms of groups of people and/or disabling conditions. Children and the elderly have been shown to benefit greatly from art therapy. This is particularly true when their ability to communicate has been inhibited by trauma, illness, or injury. In addition to their caseload, art therapists interact with a wide variety of medical and rehabilitation services professionals.

The Settings in Which Art Therapists Work

There are fewer than 1,000 art therapists in the country. Art therapists work in private offices, art rooms, or meeting rooms in facilities such as medical and psychiatric hospitals, outpatient facilities, residential treatment centers, halfway houses, shelters, schools, correctional facilities, elder-care facilities, pain clinics, universities, and art studios. The art therapist may work as part of a team that includes physicians, psychologists, nurses, rehabilitation counselors, social workers, and teachers. Together, they determine and implement a client's therapeutic, school, or mental health program. Art therapists also work as primary therapists in private practice.

Training and Other Qualifications

The basic educational requirement for an art therapist is a bachelor's degree, although a master's degree is preferred. In fact, a master's degree is required for those in private practice.

While there are a limited number of undergraduate programs in art therapy, these programs include courses in the history, theory, and practice of art therapy. They also include a supervised practicum or internship.

It is possible to prepare for a career in art therapy by following a curriculum that includes a major in either fine arts or psychology, as long as it is balanced with courses from the other area through the careful choice of electives. It is also advisable to complete courses in the life sciences. Departmental internships and cooperative education can be used to acquire the supervised experience that is expected upon graduation.

The American Art Therapy Association certifies both educational programs and art therapists. To become a certified art therapist, it is necessary to meet the educational, internship, and paid-work experience requirements. In addition, those seeking certification must present a portfolio of slides of their work and letters of recommendation.

Advancement Possibilities

Because art therapists tend to work alone or as a member of a medically oriented team, the usual paths for advancement are not possible. However, art therapists with advanced degrees may teach and do research. Others may write scholarly and technical publications to enhance their professional reputation. Those in private practice measure their advancement by the growth of their practice.

Additional Sources of Information

American Art Therapy Association, Inc.
1202 Allanson Road
Mundelein, IL 60060-3808
http://www.arttherapy.org

DANCE THERAPIST

The Nature of the Work

The goal of the dance therapist is to help clients achieve greater emotional and/or physical freedom. Like art therapists, dance therapists confer with members of a medically oriented team to determine the nature of a person's condition. The dance therapist then recommends a treatment plan and conducts programs using various forms of dance and other body movements to gain both physical and emotional responses through movement. Dance therapists instruct clients in a wide variety of movement and dance techniques.

Appraising each individual's self-expression through dance and movement can be an important part of the recovery process. As in the case of any therapist, the person's progress and regression are reported in detail to other members of the treatment team as indicators of change in the person's condition.

The People with Whom Dance Therapists Work

Dance therapy has benefited many types of patients. However, it has been recognized as an important part of the treatment plan for people diagnosed as schizophrenic or psychotic depressive. People with personality disorders also have been known to benefit from this type of therapy.

Dance therapists also treat persons with physical and learning disabilities. While some dance therapists may specialize with regard to groups and disabilities, there is such a small number of these professionals that the majority tend to be generalists working with a wide variety of people.

The Settings in Which Dance Therapists Work

There are fewer dance therapists than art therapists. Fewer than 1,000 are certified in the United States. Psychiatric hospitals and long-term mental health organizations tend to be the primary employers of dance therapists, although some work in nursing homes, adult day-care facilities, drug treatment programs, public and private schools, and private practice.

Those in private practice may have contracts with a number of health-oriented organizations. In these cases, dance therapists provide therapy for the agencies' clients as well as their own private caseload.

Training and Other Qualifications

Obviously, dance therapists are trained in a wide variety of dance forms. In addition to a strong liberal arts background at the undergraduate level, dance therapists take extensive course work in dance theory, improvisation, choreography, and kinesiology at the undergraduate level. It is also important that dance therapists have had experience teaching dance to normal populations.

This undergraduate preparation is only the foundation. In the field of dance therapy, the minimum degree requirement is a master's degree. Only 12 institutions offer the two-year master's degree program approved by the American Dance Therapy Association.

In addition to approving graduate-level programs in dance therapy, the American Dance Therapy Association also registers dance therapists who have met their criteria at two different levels. At the first level, dance therapists are registered as being qualified to work as members of a medically oriented team. At the second level of registration, dance therapists are qualified to teach, supervise, and have a private practice.

Advancement Possibilities

Like art therapists, dance therapists tend to work alone or as members of a medically oriented team. Therefore, the usual paths for advancement are not possible for them either. Dance therapists with advanced degrees and the second level of registration are qualified to teach and do research related to their field. Others may write scholarly and technical publications to enhance their professional reputation. Those in private practice gauge their professional advancement by the growth of their practice.

Additional Sources of Information

American Dance Therapy Association
2000 Century Plaza, Suite 108
10632 Little Patuxent Parkway
Columbia, MD 21044
http://www.adta.org

MUSIC THERAPIST

The Nature of the Work

Working as part of the treatment team, music therapists plan, organize, and direct musical activities and learning experiences for mentally, emotionally, and physically disabled patients. The goal of these professionals is to bring about behavioral changes that will lead patients to increased levels of awareness and understanding of themselves and their environments.

Like the other members of the rehabilitation team, music therapists collaborate with other professionals in systematically planning music activities that meet the needs, capabilities, and interests of each patient. These activities can include

- Instructing patients in instrumental or vocal music

- Directing instrumental and vocal music activities designed to benefit the patient

- Participating in instrumental and vocal music activities that benefit the patient

Music therapists also assess each patient's reaction to various experiences with music and report their observations to the entire treatment team.

The People with Whom Music Therapists Work

Music therapists work with people who have physical and mental disabilities, behavioral disorders, and learning disabilities. Music can provide an outlet for expressing deeper feelings.

Therefore, music therapy is often beneficial to people who are unable to express their feelings due to a disabling condition. Some of the groups known to benefit from music therapy include the elderly, the blind, children with learning disabilities, and cerebral palsy patients.

The Settings in Which Music Therapists Work

It is not surprising that most music therapists work in comprehensive as well as special-care hospitals, particularly psychiatric hospitals. Some work in school settings. Special-education programs benefit from the participation of a music therapist. Child and adult day-care facilities as well as nursing homes also employ music therapists.

Like dance therapists, music therapists in private practice may have service contracts with a number of organizations. However, some will maintain a private caseload in consultation with a medical, rehabilitative, or special-education team.

Training and Other Qualifications

While the educational requirements for entry into the field of music therapy are becoming more formalized, most music therapists today possess a wide range of training and experience in music, psychology, and life science. Approximately 75 colleges and universities offer undergraduate degrees in music therapy and only 12 offer master's degrees in this area. Like other therapeutic fields, certification is an important basic qualification. Therapists are certified by the National Association for Music Therapy and the American Association for Music Therapy.

The American Association for Music Therapy follows a certification process similar to that of art therapists. Music therapists not only present evidence of their educational background and supervised internship but also letters of recommendation and tapes of their music.

The National Association for Music Therapy accredits educational programs and registers graduates of those programs. The two organizations have formed an independent testing body, known as the Certification Board for Music Therapists. The board annually administers a standardized test to all candidates for certification.

Advancement Possibilities

Music therapists are not unlike art and dance therapists. They tend to work alone or as members of medically oriented teams. The traditional career path of being promoted to supervisor or director of music therapy is rarely open to them.

Music therapists with advanced degrees and certification are qualified to teach and do research. Some write scholarly and technical publications to advance the field of music therapy and enhance their own professional reputation. Those in private practice may experience an increase in the size of their practice as the quality of their work becomes known in the community.

Additional Sources of Information

American Music Therapy Association, Inc.
8455 Colesville Road, Suite 1000
Silver Spring, MD 20910
http://www.musictherapy.org

HORTICULTURAL THERAPIST

The Nature of the Work

An emerging field in rehabilitation services, horticultural therapy includes a broad range of programs that focus on vocational, social, or therapeutic outcomes for clients. Professionals in this area evaluate, rehabilitate, and train people who have mental, emotional, and/or physical disabilities. They accomplish this by using gardening activities.

In consultation with the human services or medical team, horticultural therapists teach horticulture either for vocational rehabilitation purposes or for leisure purposes. Horticultural therapists may involve a patient in a particular phase or type of gardening. In some instances the therapist may provide plant-related activities to supplement the gardening program.

Working with physicians, psychiatrists, counselors, social workers, and other therapists, horticultural therapists develop a profile of the motor skills, communication skills, health, and psychological condition of the patient. Using that data, they plan a therapy program that is appropriate for the individual. Like other therapeutic areas, they report progress and regression to the other members of the team.

The People with Whom Horticultural Therapists Work

Horticultural therapists work with a wide range of individuals who have mental and physical impairments. Participants who might be effectively treated with horticultural therapy are the mentally retarded, the emotionally disturbed, the socially maladjusted, and those with substance abuse problems.

People with physical disabilities can also be treated by horticultural therapy. These participants might be people who are blind or hearing impaired as well as victims of spinal cord injuries, stroke, heart attack, and cerebral palsy. Children with low self-esteem and the elderly have also benefited from working with a horticultural therapist.

The Settings in Which Horticultural Therapists Work

While horticultural therapists do work with individuals, they are more likely to work with their patients in groups. Generally, they work in hospitals, nursing homes, schools, vocational rehabilitation centers, drug treatment centers, juvenile detention centers, and correctional institutions. Although horticultural therapy is a relatively new therapeutic field, there are more than 1,000 programs in operation today.

Training and Other Qualifications

A bachelor's degree in horticulture or therapy/human sciences is usually required for entering this field. However, education and work experience may be combined to meet the minimum requirements for professional registration. Undergraduate programs in horticultural therapy are primarily taught in the schools of agriculture located at land grant institutions.

A typical horticultural therapy curriculum stresses not only agricultural and horticultural courses but also psychology. In addition, horticultural therapists take courses in social and behavioral sciences and horticultural therapy, and complete a supervised practicum or internship.

The American Horticultural Therapy Association registers horticultural therapists in three categories:

- **Horticultural therapist technicians.** These individuals have limited education and work experience.

- **Registered horticultural therapists.** These individuals have bachelor's degrees in horticultural therapy or related fields and have completed at least one year of paid work experience in the field.

- **Master horticultural therapists.** These individuals have completed a master's degree in horticultural therapy, have a minimum of four years of paid work experience in the field, or have demonstrated extensive educational and/or professional achievement.

Unlike most therapeutic fields, horticultural therapists are not required to be licensed by any state.

Advancement Possibilities

Horticultural therapists work as members of medically oriented teams. The traditional career path of promotion to supervisor or director is sometimes open to these employees. Advanced degrees and certification qualify them to teach and do research at colleges and universities. As is true of many art, music, and dance therapists, some horticultural therapists write scholarly and technical publications to advance the field and enhance their professional reputation.

Additional Sources of Information

American Horticultural Therapy Association
909 York Street
Denver, CO 80206
http://www.ahta.org

RECREATION THERAPIST

The Nature of the Work

Recreation therapists are other possible members of treatment teams. Their special role on such teams is to foster, educate, and encourage patients to participate in leisure activities. These activities are designed to facilitate the patient's recovery or adjustment to an illness, injury, disability, or emotional condition.

Therapeutic recreation specialists have the responsibility for planning, organizing, and directing recreation programs that have been medically approved. The programs can include adapted sports, games, arts, crafts, music, field trips, and social activities. The content of each program is determined in consultation with other members of the treatment team after the recreation therapist assesses a patient's talents, interests, and current abilities.

The primary purpose of the recreation therapist's work is either to restore a prior level of skill or to develop new leisure skills and activities. This is important to the overall recovery process because the recreation therapist is able to help that patient attain not only a skill but also a quality of life that is personally satisfying.

Like other members of the treatment team, recreation therapists must prepare detailed reports. These reports describe each patient's reactions to the planned activities. They may also include physical and emotional symptoms that manifest themselves before, during, or after participation in an activity. Other therapies and/or the recreational activities may need to be adapted or changed in response to the patient's reactions.

The People with Whom Recreation Therapists Work

Recreation therapists work with patients recovering from physical and mental illness. They may be children, teenagers, or adults. In addition, recreation therapists work with the elderly and provide them with opportunities for exercise, mental stimulation, creativity, and fun.

Special populations such as the terminally ill, the blind, the hearing impaired, children with learning disabilities, substance abusers, prison inmates, and juvenile offenders may also be served by recreation therapists. As in other therapeutic career fields, recreation therapists tend to specialize in treating certain groups and/or disabilities. Because much of their work is carried out as group activities, specialization is very important.

The Settings in Which Recreation Therapists Work

The majority of recreation therapists work in comprehensive hospitals or in psychiatric hospitals. An increasing number are working in nursing homes and residential facilities. Recreation therapists are also employed in community mental health centers, adult day-care programs, local parks and recreation departments, special education programs, drug treatment centers, and correctional institutions.

A few recreation therapists are self-employed. They work under contract with organizations such as nursing homes or community agencies. They either provide recreation therapy for the organization's clients or they develop and oversee programs for the agencies.

Training and Other Qualifications

The basic requirement for entering the field of recreation therapy is a bachelor's degree in therapeutic recreation or in recreation with a concentration in therapeutic recreation. These programs of study require course work in human anatomy, physiology, abnormal psychology, medical and psychiatric terminology, characteristics of illnesses and disabilities, the concepts of mainstreaming and normalization, professional ethics, and assessment and referral procedures. In addition, recreation therapists take courses in therapeutic recreation theory and practice, program design and management, professional issues, and a 360-hour clinical internship under the direct supervision of a certified recreation therapist.

The National Council for Therapeutic Recreation Certification is the organization that certifies recreation therapists and therapeutic recreation assistants. Certified recreation therapists must hold at least a bachelor's degree in recreation therapy and pass the certification examination. Therapeutic recreation assistants must hold at least an associate's degree.

The council also accredits undergraduate and graduate programs of study in colleges and universities. There are more than 60 accredited programs in the United States.

Advancement Possibilities

While most recreation therapists work as members of a medically oriented team, experienced recreation therapists can become supervisors and directors of recreation therapy in hospitals, clinics, and agency programs. If they are employed in a small hospital or clinic, they can move to larger organizations.

A few recreation therapists move from salaried positions in hospitals to private practice. As in the case of physical and occupational therapists, this trend is expected to increase as many agencies begin to use contract services to provide specialized health-care delivery. Recreation therapists with advanced degrees also teach and do research in higher education.

Additional Sources of Information   American Therapeutic Recreation Association
1414 Prince Street, Suite 204
Alexandria, VA 22314
http://www.atra-tr.org

National Council for Therapeutic Recreation Certification
7 Elmwood Drive
New City, NY 10956
http://www.nctrc.org

National Therapeutic Recreation Society
22377 Belmont Ridge Road
Ashburn, VA 20148
http://www.nrpa.org/branches/ntrs.htm

SPEECH-LANGUAGE PATHOLOGIST AND AUDIOLOGIST

Some people are born with hearing and/or speech disorders. Others suffer loss of hearing or speech as a result of illness, injury, or severe emotional stress. Speech-language pathologists and audiologists are the professionals who work with them.

The Nature of the Work   **Speech-language pathologists** diagnose and treat people who have communication problems. These problems can include hearing loss, an inability to make speech sounds or understand language, stuttering, poor and irregular rhythm and fluency, and improper pitch. Some speech-language pathologists also work with individuals who have difficulty eating and swallowing.

Using special instrumentation and other testing devices, professionals in this area evaluate speech and language skills. In addition they design, direct, and implement treatment plans to restore or improve a patient's communication ability. This may include counseling people with speech and language disabilities or serving as a consultant to educational or medical professionals who are important to the patient's rehabilitation.

Audiologists diagnose and treat people with hearing disorders. They evaluate the range, nature, and degree of hearing loss using special instrumentation such as audiometers. Like the speech-language pathologists, audiologists design, direct, and implement treatment plans to improve the patient's hearing. Audiologists fit patients for hearing aids and other mechanical devices to improve their hearing ability. Audiologists also counsel their patients about their disability and the treatment they are receiving. They also serve as consultants to educational, medical, and other professional groups central to the patient's rehabilitation.

Some professionals in this area are trained in both speech-language pathology and audiology because the relationship between hearing and speech-language disorders is very strong. This combination of training allows these professionals to provide a complete treatment program for the patient.

Others in the fields of speech-language pathology and audiology may teach the scientific principles of human hearing and communication. Others may direct projects and conduct research in the areas of speech and hearing loss. These activities may be directed at developing new instrumentation to aid in the diagnosis of disorders. They may also be directed at the development of new equipment and instrumentation to help diagnose or restore all or part of a patient's hearing or speech loss.

The People with Whom Speech-Language Pathologists and Audiologists Work

Speech-language pathologists and audiologists usually specialize. There are many who work with children. But increasingly there is a growing demand for these professionals to work with the elderly.

Some speech-language pathologists specialize in the treatment of certain communication disorders such as stuttering or total speech loss due to injury or illness. Likewise, audiologists also specialize in terms of the type of hearing disorder.

Speech-language pathologists and audiologists work in consultation with other professionals and the families of their patients. Because so many speech-language pathologists and audiologists work with children, they must maintain strong relationships with teachers and parents who will continue to help the child progress between treatment sessions.

The Settings in Which Speech-Language Pathologists and Audiologists Work

The majority of speech-language pathologists and audiologists work in the public or private school setting. From preschool to college, these professionals work with educators, doctors, and parents to facilitate learning for children with hearing and speech-language disorders.

A smaller percentage work in hospitals, speech-language and hearing centers, and home health-care agencies. Some work in doctor's offices. Still others have a private practice either alone or with other professionals.

Training and Other Qualifications

A master's degree in speech-language or audiology is a requirement in this field, although people with a bachelor's degree in speech-language pathology may become certified as special-education teachers by state educational agencies. However, federal law requires that speech-language pathologists within a school setting have a master's degree.

The master's degree and supervised clinical experience, a passing score on a national examination, and nine months of experience after graduation are required for state licensure in most states. This training also qualifies the professional for certification by the American Speech-Language-Hearing Association. The certification is called the Certificate of Clinical Competency (CCC). Some professionals become certified in either speech-language pathology or in audiology. Increasingly, new professionals are seeking certification in both areas.

**Advancement
Possibilities**

As speech-language pathologists and audiologists gain experience, they often move from salaried positions in school systems and hospitals to private practice. This trend is expected to increase as public agencies downsize their staff and use contract services to provide health-care delivery.

Other speech-language pathologists and audiologists become directors and administrators of programs in schools, hospitals, and health-care or government agencies. Those with advanced degrees teach and do research in colleges and universities.

**Additional Sources of
Information**

American Speech-Language-Hearing Association
10801 Rockville Pike
Rockville, MD 20852
http://www.asha.org

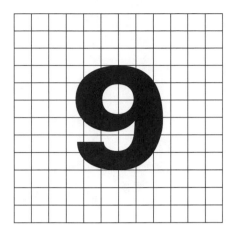

EDUCATIONAL SERVICES

The professionals represented in this chapter are important members of the educational staff of a wide variety of schools, colleges, and universities. They work not only with the students but with the parents, teachers, administrators, and community agencies to facilitate the academic and personal development of children and young adults.

The people in educational services occupations have much in common. All of them

- Work in educational settings
- Are concerned about the education and overall well-being of children and young adults
- Deal with personal, social, academic, and/or career problems

While their settings, students, and techniques may differ, they are committed to the learning process. Their responsibilities can include direct client services, program administration, and/or special instruction.

The settings can include public and private elementary, middle, and high schools; special-education facilities; rehabilitation and vocational centers; other special schools; and colleges and universities.

Some professionals work exclusively with preschool children. Others work with children with learning disabilities, children who are exhibiting antisocial behavior, or children who have been the victims of crime. Still others work with college students. Consequently, there is a wide variety of parent and teacher situations in which these professionals work and interact.

The occupations in this chapter represent an opportunity for people who are interested in both rehabilitation services careers and the education of students to combine their interests and abilities. Some of these occupations also allow individuals to enter with a bachelor's degree. However, advancement in almost all of these occupations requires advanced degrees and numerous years of experience.

SCHOOL PSYCHOLOGIST

The Nature of the Work
While the field of psychology offers a wide variety of career options, one of the more important is the school psychologist. School psychologists are members of the educational team who have an in-depth understanding of human intelligence and who have the expertise to measure mental capacity. Therefore, their role in the educational system generally focuses on diagnostic and remedial work with a wide range of special students.

School psychologists become involved in diagnosing children with learning disabilities as well as gifted and talented students. They work with parents, teachers, and children to facilitate the educational success of both types of special children.

In addition, school psychologists deal with the social and emotional condition of children. They may use individual or group counseling sessions to help students cope with learning, behavioral, and emotional problems. They may also work in consultation with classroom teachers and parents to continue the progress being made in the counseling sessions.

Training and Other Qualifications
A master's degree in school or counseling psychology is a minimum qualification for the position of school psychologist. Some school psychologists even hold doctoral degrees. While it is not a necessary qualification, in almost every field of psychology, a doctorate is highly recommended. In some cases, it may also be important that the school psychologist graduate from a program approved by the American Psychological Association (APA). Some positions in large, urban school systems can require graduation from an APA-accredited institution.

Advancement Possibilities
Because most school psychologists are the only mental health professionals in their school setting, advancement to supervisor or director within the school is not possible. However, some school psychologists move from a small school to a larger one, and others move to supervisory positions within their school district or state.

Those with doctoral degrees can teach and do research at colleges and universities. Those who become licensed psychologists may enter private practice and specialize in the educational and developmental problems of school-children.

Additional Sources of Information

American Psychological Association
750 First Street NE, Suite 100
Washington, DC 20002
http://www.apa.org

Association of State and Provincial Psychology Boards
P.O. Box 241245
Montgomery, AL 36124-1245
http://www.asppb.org

National Association of School Psychologists
4340 East West Highway, Suite 402
Bethesda, MD 20814
http://www.naspweb.org

SCHOOL SOCIAL WORKER

The Nature of the Work

Like psychology, the field of social work offers a wide variety of career options. School social workers deal with the problems of children in elementary, middle, or high school. They assist parents, teachers, and students in developing permanent solutions and/or coping strategies for these children to make them more able to learn.

School social workers play an important role in gathering data about the students with whom they work and the circumstances in which they live. They prepare family histories and interview all parties who play a significant role in the life of their students. School social workers can become involved in such issues as child abuse and neglect, teenage pregnancy, date rape, family conflicts, antisocial behavior, substance abuse, physical and mental disabilities, learning problems, illness, and poverty.

Using direct counseling and referral techniques, school social workers identify and consider solutions. They also find resources and information to improve the overall quality of life for children so that they can get the most from their educational experiences. Like other types of social workers, school social workers have to value the dignity and worth of each student and build a basis for trust and understanding.

Training and Other Qualifications

While a bachelor's degree in social work may be a sufficient requirement for a small, rural school system, most social workers who are employed in public school systems must have a master's degree in social work. The graduate program of study that school social workers follow includes courses in human growth and development, social welfare policies, and methods of social work.

The master's degree for social workers interested in working in a school setting requires at least one year of experience in such a setting under the direct supervision of an experienced M.S.W. After two years of supervised experience as paid social workers, these professionals are eligible for membership in the Academy of Certified Social Workers.

Advancement Possibilities

Like school psychologists, a school social worker is usually the only social worker on the school staff. Therefore, advancement to supervisory positions within the school is rare. Those with the proper education and experience can be promoted to supervisor of school social workers for a district or for the state. It is also possible to move from a small school to a larger one and assume more responsibility.

Additional Sources of Information

Council on Social Work Education
1725 Duke Street, Suite 500
Alexandria, VA 22314
(Publishes the *Directory of Accredited B.S.W. and M.S.W. Programs*)
http://www.cswe.org

National Association of Social Workers
750 First Street NE, Suite 700
Washington, DC 20002-4241
http://www.naswdc.org

SCHOOL COUNSELOR

The Nature of the Work

School counselors are an important part of the educational community. While they assist students in dealing with personal, family, and social problems, they also help students learn the skills needed to deal with problems before they occur. They assist students with their educational and career decisions. Their primary goal is to enhance the personal, social, and academic growth of each student with whom they work.

To achieve this goal, school counselors emphasize preventive and developmental counseling by using a wide variety of strategies to work with their students. They interview students to assess personal needs, interests, and abilities. They conduct individual and group counseling sessions. They administer and interpret aptitude, interest, personality, and achievement tests. They also teach skills that help students manage their time better, conduct a more successful job search, prepare for interviews at colleges and universities as well as with employers, and reduce their level of test anxiety.

At the elementary school level, counselors often deal with social, behavioral, and personal problems on an individual basis. At the high school level, school counselors continue to deal with these issues on either an individual basis or in groups. But at the high school level, counselors become increasingly more involved in assisting students as they make decisions about their future. These may include such important issues as employment upon graduation, selection of an appropriate college and major, and/or marriage and family decisions.

School counselors consult with parents, teachers, school administrators, school psychologists, school nurses, and social workers. They also make referrals to medical, psychological, community, and law enforcement agencies.

Training and Other Qualifications

School counselors must have a master's degree in guidance and counseling or a master's degree in either elementary or secondary school counseling. In some cases, school counselors are required to have a number of years of teaching experience prior to becoming a school counselor. In addition, more than half of all states require that school counselors be licensed, certified, or registered in order to work in the public school system.

The graduate course work that school counselors complete includes human growth and development, social and cultural foundations, helping relationships, individual and group counseling techniques, occupational information and career counseling, individual appraisal, and research and evaluation. School counselors also take courses in the history and philosophy of education. Graduate programs in counseling are usually accredited by the Council for Accreditation of Counseling and Related Educational Programs.

Advancement Possibilities

School counselors at large public and private schools that have several counselors on staff can become directors of guidance. They can also be promoted to directors or supervisors of guidance for their school, district, or state. Some school counselors may move from small schools to larger schools where their responsibilities may be expanded.

School counselors who pass state licensing requirements and become certified by the National Board for Certified Counselors may enter private practice. Often they will specialize in treating the problems of schoolchildren. Those who obtain a doctorate can become counselor educators who teach and conduct research at universities. Others consult with educators and business.

Additional Sources of Information

American Counseling Association
5999 Stevenson Avenue
Alexandria, VA 22304
http://www.counseling.org

American School Counselor Association
5999 Stevenson Avenue
Alexandria, VA 22304
http://www.schoolcounselor.org

Council for Accreditation of Counseling and Related Educational Programs
c/o American Counseling Association
5999 Stevenson Avenue
Alexandria, VA 22304
http://www.counseling.org/cacrep

National Board for Certified Counselors
3 Terrace Way, Suite D
Greensboro, NC 27403
http://www.nbcc.org

COLLEGE STUDENT AFFAIRS PROFESSIONAL

The Nature of the Work College student affairs professionals deal with all phases of college life beyond the classroom. Some of the types of positions that might be classified under this occupational field include the following:

Dean of students. This person administers college or university policy that pertains primarily to student services and student behavior. The dean of students also plans, implements, and evaluates programs designed to provide services to the student body. In general, other student affairs professionals report to the dean of students. In some cases, the dean of students may also have the title of vice president for student affairs. In large colleges and universities, these tend to be two different positions.

Placement counselor. This person assists students and alumni in obtaining jobs in their career field. Placement counselors work with business and industry as well as with the students and faculty. They set up campus interviews and prepare students for the job search process.

Counselors. These professionals provide services to students who are experiencing adjustment problems, emotional problems, and/or academic difficulties.

Resident hall coordinators. These people oversee campus life in the dormitories. Their responsibilities can include assigning rooms, training volunteer resident hall advisors, planning educational and social programs, and dealing with emergencies that occur.

Student center personnel. These people manage campus student centers, which often contain dining facilities, bookstores, recreational facilities, meeting rooms, and student organization offices. Some positions in student centers are strictly administrative. They deal with such issues as policy, budget, and personnel. Other positions are programmatic. They deal with the planning and implementation of special student programs and events.

Student advisers. These people advise special groups of students on personal, social, and academic matters. They supplement the work of the student's academic adviser who is generally a faculty member responsible for advising the student on appropriate courses to take. These special student advisers work with certain groups of students such as foreign students, minority students, female students, adult students, disabled students, and sorority and fraternity members.

Financial aid counselors. These people assist students in obtaining federal, state, local, and institutional funding to pursue their education.

Admissions officers. These people review the applications to attend the college or university and make decisions with regard to who will be admitted each year.

Registrar. This person maintains the academic records of all students. This record includes all of the grades that a student has received throughout his or her college career. It may also include any disciplinary actions taken against the student.

Training and Other Qualifications

The minimum requirement for a position in college student affairs is a bachelor's degree. However, a bachelor's degree greatly limits a person's career options on any college campus. Most college student affairs professionals hold a master's degree in higher education administration, counseling, educational psychology, or some related area. Those with doctoral degrees tend to hold upper-level administrative positions or counseling positions. There are no licensing or certification requirements for college student affairs professionals. However, members of college counseling centers may be graduates of doctoral programs in psychology, which are approved by the American Psychological Association. In addition, these counselors may be licensed psychologists in the state where they practice.

Advancement Possibilities

In many areas of college student affairs work there is real opportunity for career progression. Coordinator or assistant positions generally require only a bachelor's degree upon entry. However, with increased levels of experience and education, which is often available at the institution with a tuition waiver, it is possible to advance to counseling and administrative positions.

People with doctorates and numerous years of experience are qualified for the highest levels of college administration. They may also teach and do research as part of the college or university faculty. Some student affairs professionals go to federal or state government positions in departments of education.

Additional Sources of Information

American College Counseling Association
5999 Stevenson Avenue
Alexandria, VA 22304
http://www.collegecounseling.org

American College Personnel Association
One Dupont Circle, Suite 300
Washington, DC 20036
http://www.acpa.nche.edu

American Counseling Association
5999 Stevenson Avenue
Alexandria, VA 22304
http://www.counseling.org

National Association of Colleges and Employers
(formerly College Placement Council)
62 Highland Avenue
Bethlehem, PA 18017-9085
http://www.naceweb.org

SPECIAL SERVICES

By now it is obvious that careers in rehabilitation services are diverse in their responsibilities, their settings, the people they serve, the training that is required, and the patterns of advancement. While some occupations are easily grouped in employment services, mental health services, medical services, therapeutic services, and educational services, there are some that provide unique possibilities. This chapter offers a brief overview of some of these unique occupations.

CHRISTIAN CLERGY AND JEWISH RABBINATE

From the beginning of time there have been people who served the spiritual needs of children and adults. In our society these people are primarily ministers, priests, and rabbis. They hold a special place in the community because of the counsel and comfort they provide.

The Nature of the Work Religious leaders of all faiths conduct regular worship services and administer religious rites, such as weddings and funerals, in accordance with the teachings of their faith. They also counsel members of their congregations who are in need of spiritual advice. In addition, they teach and interpret the doctrine of their religion through sermons and religious education classes. They bring comfort to the sick; likewise, bereaved members of the congregation look to the clergy or the rabbi for counsel during their times of loss and anguish.

Some religious leaders publish their interpretations of the faith in books and articles. Others participate in interfaith organizations as well as civic, educational, and recreational activities.

The Settings in Which the Clergy and Rabbinate Work

Most clergy and rabbis work in synagogues, churches, or parishes. Some work as missionaries, taking the teachings of their faith to many parts of the world. Others work as chaplains in the military, in hospitals, and on college campuses. Some teach in universities and in seminaries.

Training and Other Qualifications

Every religion has a unique program to prepare those who plan to enter a religious vocation. The content of each program varies, but all clergy and rabbis must have a thorough knowledge of the beliefs and practices of their faith.

Some preparation can take three to five years. At the conclusion, a bachelor's degree is awarded. In other cases, there are no formal requirements. Many people who plan to enter the religious profession begin by learning the basic teachings of their faith early in life. Others come to the realization that they have a calling to religious life as adults. Sometimes these individuals have education and careers in very different fields. It is then necessary for them to complete a formal program of religious education.

Advancement Possibilities

The traditional concept of advancement in a career field may appear inappropriate when discussing religious vocations. However, new ministers, priests, and rabbis usually begin by assisting another rabbi or clergy member. With experience, they may assume more responsibility for their congregations.

Within each religion there is a hierarchy of religious leadership. In addition to embodying the values of the faith, those who reach higher levels of spiritual leadership within their faith usually have advanced training or education as well as experience.

Additional Sources of Information

Hebrew Union College
Jewish Institute of Religion
One West Fourth Street
New York, NY 10012

Jewish Theological Seminary of America
3080 Broadway
New York, NY 10027
http://www.jtsa.edu

National Coalition for Church Vocations
5420 South Cornell Avenue #105
Chicago, IL 60615-5604
http://www.nccv-vocations.org

PROBATION OFFICER/PAROLE OFFICER

The Nature of the Work Probation and parole officers are a unique group of social workers who participate in the formulation and development of plans to release juvenile and adult offenders from correctional institutions. They provide supervision for offenders who have been released, and they develop a regular plan of treatment and follow-up during the time of probation or parole.

Probation and parole officers secure necessary services for offenders including education and employment. They also make referrals to other social services agencies and rehabilitation services professionals who provide necessary services to offenders.

It is important that a probation or parole officer establish a good working relationship with the offender to gain a thorough understanding of his or her personal history before, during, and after incarceration. Working with the family of the offender can also be an important part of rehabilitation.

Probation and parole officers also make recommendations to the courts on sentencing and parole. They can return an offender to a correctional institution if the individual is not adhering to the conditions of his or her parole or probation.

The traditional casework methods of social work are very important in this occupation. Direct counseling, securing services, making referrals, and conducting follow-up are all important tasks performed by probation and parole officers.

The Settings in Which Probation Officers/ Parole Officers Work Probation and parole officers work for the court system. Generally, they are employed by correctional institutions or parole agencies.

Training and Other Qualifications A bachelor's degree in social work, rehabilitation services, sociology, psychology, or another social science is good preparation for a career as a probation or parole officer.

Advancement Possibilities Probation and parole officers are able to advance to supervisory positions. Those with the proper education and experience can be promoted to direct an agency. It is also possible for probation and parole officers to move from a small agency to a larger one and assume more responsibility.

Additional Sources of Information National Council on Crime and Delinquency
685 Market Street, Suite 620
San Francisco, CA 94105
http://www.cascomm.com/users/nccd/

REHABILITATION AIDES

The field of rehabilitation services offers numerous opportunities to work as **aides** in a wide variety of occupations and settings. Aide positions are very accessible for those who want to be part of the rehabilitation services career field but do not have the experience and/or the educational requirements for professional positions.

Rehabilitation aide positions generally do not have a specific education requirement. Employers prefer at least some high school education, and a high school diploma is considered very helpful if the position is a full-time one.

There is a growing demand for rehabilitation services. As the population ages, as people with disabilities enter the mainstream of American life, and as educators take on the responsibility of educating the whole child, there will be an increasing demand for people who can assist the professionals in the field. Therefore, the number of aide positions is expected to grow in the future. The following are only a few of the possibilities that exist for rehabilitation aides.

Geriatric Aide

In this highly rewarding but demanding job, geriatric aides assist and care for the elderly. Geriatric aides work with rehabilitation services professionals who specialize in caring for the elderly, whose conditions can range from critically ill to relatively healthy. The professionals with whom geriatric aides work include doctors, nurses, physical therapists, occupational therapists, speech specialists, nutritionists, recreation specialists, social workers, and rehabilitation counselors.

The responsibilities of a geriatric aide can include feeding, bathing, dressing, and accompanying the elderly. Some geriatric aides monitor the medical status of elderly patients. Others assist in recreational activities.

The duties of geriatric aides are as varied as the settings in which those duties are carried out. Aides work in medical, therapeutic, recreational, and transportation settings. They can be employed in hospitals, nursing homes, adult day-care centers, recreational programs, and private homes.

There are new and emerging college degree programs that focus on working with the elderly. There are also graduate programs that prepare people to direct gerontology programs. A person can begin as a geriatric aide and with time, experience, and advanced education can assume increasing amounts of responsibility in this growing field.

To advance from the position of geriatric aide, it is necessary to pursue additional education in a related area. Nursing school can prepare a person to be a geriatric nurse. A bachelor's degree in areas such as social work, rehabilitation services, psychology, or sociology can open a wide variety of options, including medical school. Specialized training can also lead to positions as a medical assistant.

Additional Sources of Information

American Geriatrics Society
Empire State Building
350 Fifth Avenue, Suite 801
New York, NY 10118
http://www.americangeriatrics.org

Psychiatric Aide

Psychiatric aides have demanding positions, but these can be highly rewarding jobs. Through their day-to-day activities in helping patients with their personal care or assisting them in getting to and from their treatments and activities, psychiatric aides are often the ones to see a patient experience small personal triumphs.

Under the close supervision of the professional staff, psychiatric aides measure vital statistics, collect laboratory specimens, draw blood, administer medications, and perform other routine nursing procedures. They help patients and their families adjust to hospitalization. They motivate and encourage the patient to follow the treatment plan and to participate in activities that the medical team has prescribed.

They are important to the professional team because they observe and record important information on the reactions and symptoms of the patients. It is often the psychiatric aide who first observes important changes in behavior. Therefore, psychiatric aides need to be very good at record keeping.

Psychiatric aides primarily work in psychiatric hospitals and the psychiatric units of large hospitals. Some work in community mental health programs, residential facilities, nursing homes, and drug treatment centers.

While a high school diploma is not required, often the psychiatric aide receives training on the job. These training programs can last a few days or a few months. Some community colleges offer courses that prepare psychiatric aides. The course work in these programs includes anatomy, physiology, medical terminology, nutrition, and communication skills.

To advance from the position of psychiatric aide, it is necessary to pursue additional education. Some psychiatric aides go on to nursing school, while others go on to college and obtain an undergraduate degree in an area such as psychology, social work, or rehabilitation services. Some continue their education in graduate programs such as counseling, psychology, or social work; others go on to medical school.

Physical and Occupational Therapy Aides

Working with physical and occupational therapists, these aides prepare patients for their treatments. They also assist during the administration of the treatments by adjusting equipment, encouraging the patient, and securing the patient in specialized equipment. In some cases, physical and occupational therapy aides may provide routine treatment, but they always work under the close supervision of a licensed certified therapist.

Like other aides, physical and occupational therapy aides work very closely with patients. They assist them in dressing and in removing or putting on prosthetic or orthotic devices. As the patients practice their exercises, the aides observe and record data on the results of the treatment.

Physical and occupational therapy aides maintain an inventory of equipment and supplies. They are also responsible for keeping the equipment clean and in working order.

Aides in this field work side by side with the physical or occupational therapist. Therefore, they work in hospitals and rehabilitation centers. However, more aides will be needed in home health agencies, nursing homes, hospices, sports medicine centers, athletic departments of colleges and universities, and fitness programs in business and industry as the demand for therapists in these settings increases. Physical and occupational therapists in private practice may employ aides to work with them as well.

During high school, the best preparation for becoming a physical or occupational therapy aide is course work in biology and psychology. This is also good preparation for continuing one's education beyond high school as a means to advance to the position of a physical or occupational therapist.

CAREER PATHS AND UPWARD MOBILITY IN REHABILITATION SERVICES

The rehabilitation services field offers many different career paths and many different rewards. The appropriate path depends on the occupation you select and on your personal interests, abilities, needs, and values. However, there are five basic traits that successful individuals in any field exhibit:

1. Setting long-range goals but not dwelling on them

2. Taking the possibility of failure for granted and not worrying about it

3. Avoiding self-intimidation by not setting grandiose goals and over-whelming challenges

4. Not setting limited work hours

5. Verbally attributing achievements to "luck" but inwardly holding a strong belief in their power to overcome challenges

These traits are as true for rehabilitation services careers as any other career field. While some occupations within the field of rehabilitation services do not offer what is commonly thought of as "career progression," the traits of successful people will probably result in career success however the occupation or individual defines it.

For example, new professionals who enter a particular field, such as art therapy, may not be able to anticipate being promoted from a staff position to a supervisory and then to an executive position. Their success will be defined in terms of professional reputation and an expanding practice. However, in other areas of rehabilitation services, "promotion" may be a realistic expectation.

Movement between agencies is a common path to higher-level responsibility. In addition, many occupations within rehabilitation services offer the ability to enter private practice. This is another career path that many people in rehabilitation services follow. It is important to look at the types of career paths that are available. However, the basic keys to career mobility and advancement in the field of rehabilitation services are education, experience, and certification and licensure.

PATHS TO CLINICAL CAREERS

The chapters on mental health services, medical services, and therapeutic services each describe clinical occupations in the rehabilitation services field. These occupations all demand education beyond the bachelor's degree. In some cases, a master's degree is the minimum level of education required for entry. In other cases, a doctorate or professional degree, such as a medical degree, is required.

However, education alone is not sufficient for people entering clinical careers. They must also have years of supervised clinical experience under the direction of other certified and licensed professionals. In some fields this is paid, supervised experience and in other fields it is unpaid. It is important to gather all of the information available on the nature and duration of the clinical experience that is required in your area of interest.

Clinical careers all demand the passing of a certification examination and, in many cases, a separate licensing examination. These examinations are administered by both professional organizations in the field and licensing boards in the states where the individual plans to practice.

Because the public places such a high degree of trust in rehabilitation services professionals who pursue clinical careers, there is a demanding process for entry and advancement. This is a necessary protection for both the public and the professional. Once certified and licensed, it is imperative that you continue to take courses on a regular basis to stay current in your field and to renew the certification and licensing on a regular basis.

PATHS TO ADMINISTRATIVE CAREERS

The key to pursuing an administrative career in rehabilitation services is obtaining the proper education. Generally this is a master's degree in an area such as:

- Rehabilitation counseling

- General counseling

- Mental health counseling

- Social work

- Counseling psychology

- Sociology

These graduate programs do not actually prepare students to work as administrators. The emphasis is almost exclusively in the area of counseling theory and technique. However, career advancement in the area of administration can be very rapid upon completion of a master's degree, particularly a rehabilitation counseling degree. Studies have shown that within as few as 18 months of completing a master's in rehabilitation counseling, a significant percentage of people are promoted to supervisory or administrative positions. The vast majority of these graduates reach managerial positions within less than five years of graduation.

In supervisory positions the responsibilities may still be very closely related to the delivery of patient/client services. A supervisor of rehabilitation counseling or social work counselors will generally be responsible for a staff of other counselors and social workers who provide individual and group counseling services to the patients/clients.

Supervisory responsibilities are quite different from those of the agency director, even though both may hold the same degree in counseling or social work. The director or agency administrator is responsible for such areas as fiscal management, program planning and evaluation, public relations, and marketing services. He or she also has ultimate responsibility for managing counseling and noncounseling personnel. The size of the agency plays a significant part in determining the amount of contact the director or administrator has with clients/patients.

Decisions about career advancement in administrative positions in rehabilitation services fields are often made by the agency's board of directors. Studies have shown that these boards tend to evaluate candidates for administrative positions on six major criteria:

1. Prior experience in management and supervision

2. An academic degree appropriate to the agency's mission and goals (This is usually a master's degree but sometimes a doctorate is preferred.)

3. A history of career advancement with evidence of leadership skills and initiative

4. A stable employment history

5. Evidence of interest in the mission and goals of the agency through paid or volunteer experience

6. A well-conducted interview for the position and excellent references

GRADUATE AND PROFESSIONAL EDUCATION

The field of rehabilitation services offers a wide range of opportunities, from aides to physicians. However, graduate or professional education is the real key to career mobility, if not advancement, in this field. To determine if you should be planning to pursue a graduate or professional degree, ask yourself the following questions:

Do I have a real interest in the subject I am planning to study?

Am I trying to advance my skills in this particular area?

Do I have a real desire to help others?

Does my career field require graduate education?

If you can answer yes to one or more of these questions, the next step is to select a college or university with the type of graduate/professional program that suits your needs. There are numerous directories of colleges and universities that will give you a listing of the institutions and the types of programs that they offer.

Identifying Graduate and Professional Programs

A good directory will provide information on such things as the faculty/student ratio (it should be low), the number of master's and doctoral degrees awarded annually, the percentage of women and minorities admitted, whom to contact for application materials, and the list of standardized tests that are required.

Standardized Tests and Graduate or Professional School

While medical schools require the Medical College Admissions Test (MCAT), graduate programs in most other areas of rehabilitation services require the Graduate Record Examination (GRE) or the Miller's Analogies Test (MAT). It is advisable to take these tests during your senior year of college, even if you are not planning to go on to graduate school. The scores are good for five years, and many people have changed their plans and decided to go to graduate school after being out of college a few years. It is difficult to review all of the material, particularly the mathematics portion of the exam, when you have not been in school for several years.

Completing the Application

Graduate applications usually require basic information about you and your undergraduate record. The application package includes:

- An application form

- An official transcript of your undergraduate courses and grades

- Usually three letters of reference, preferably from faculty members who can comment on your academic ability

- A statement of purpose—why you want to pursue graduate study and what you have to offer to the program

- Your request for financial assistance

Unlike undergraduate admissions, which are reviewed and evaluated in the admissions office, graduate applications are reviewed and evaluated by the faculty members who will teach you and work with you. Therefore, before you apply it is advisable to learn all you can about the faculty in the department. Where are their degrees from? What is their area of expertise? What books and articles have they published? Are they interested in the same things that interest you? These are important questions.

Paying for Graduate or Professional School

There can be more options available for graduate students than undergraduate students when it comes to paying for graduate programs. While student loans are available to graduate students, there are often other sources of financial assistance that are unique to graduate study, including:

Teaching assistantships. These provide stipends, and sometimes tuition waivers, to full-time graduate students for assisting a faculty member in teaching undergraduate classes.

Research assistantships. These provide stipends, and sometimes tuition waivers, to full-time graduate students for assistance on a faculty research project.

Fellowships. These provide money to full-time graduate students to cover the costs of study and living expenses and are not based on an obligation to assist in teaching or conducting research.

In most graduate programs, these forms of financial assistance are very competitive. It is important to have a good undergraduate record and evidence of a commitment to the field. The commitment can be evidenced in the form of paid related work experience or volunteer experience. The faculty committee that reviews applications for this type of financial assistance needs to see that you can make a substantive contribution to their work.

HOW TO IDENTIFY ORGANIZATIONAL CULTURES

Upon completion of your education or training program you will enter an organization or agency that will have its own unique culture. The staff members will have a way in which they communicate, both formally and informally. This form of communication may be different among peers than it is with supervisors and administrators. As the new person on staff, you may have very little power to change this culture; therefore, it is important to assess the environment before accepting the position. If you don't, you greatly increase the probability of failure on the job should your values and the culture of the organization clash.

There will be indications of the culture in the description of the job for which you apply and in the way they describe their organization or agency during the interview. Do they emphasize a team approach or independent work? Do they demonstrate a basic respect for their clients/patients? Are their mission and their goals compatible with their programs or treatments? What is the turnover rate of their professional staff? Do they promote from within?

These are some of the issues you will want to assess. You will also want to meet with as many professional staff people as possible during your initial, or subsequent, interview to determine if there is a good fit between you and the organization. When you are asked if you have any questions, be prepared! It is then your turn to evaluate the employer. Ask such questions as

What are the opportunities for personal growth?

Could you describe a typical career path in this agency?

How will I be evaluated?

What is the turnover rate of the position for which I am being considered?

What are the agency's plans for the future?

Is the agency stable and financially sound?

What makes your agency different from others that do the same thing?

Describe the management style of your organization.

Describe the work environment.

Why do you enjoy working here?

What characteristics does a person need to be successful here?

Keep in mind that the most important aspect of personal and professional growth is a positive mental attitude about yourself: your strengths, your weaknesses, your skills, your abilities, and your interests. This is the fundamental building block of any successful career. When you have a clear picture of your own potential, it is easier to plan and pursue a career that is compatible with your interests and abilities as well as your needs and values.

PROFESSIONAL LICENSURE AND CERTIFICATION

All rehabilitation services professionals have a legal obligation to perform their professional duties in a manner that is the same as all other professionals in the field. Any professional who fails to do this when providing services to clients/patients can be legally charged with malpractice or negligence.

In these instances, the court or the jury will determine whether or not the professional standard of care was breached. In most cases the "standard of care" is set by the appropriate professional organization and/or the state's licensing board for the particular occupation.

Laws and regulations concerning all forms of rehabilitation services have drastically increased within the last decade. For this reason, clients/patients are expecting more and better services from rehabilitation services professionals. People entering any occupation in this field should not only be well prepared in terms of theory and technique but also in terms of the federal and state laws that pertain to the standards of care for that particular occupation.

In addition, it is advisable to become familiar with the ethical standards and guidelines that are prepared by the professional organizations in the appropriate field. These are easily available by writing to the appropriate organization.

In almost all areas of rehabilitation services, licensure and certification assure the public, and other professionals, that those holding such credentials are knowledgeable of and subscribe to the professional standards of care for their particular occupation. In some occupations it is not possible to be employed without these credentials.

WHAT IS LICENSURE?

Most states have established licensure boards to preserve the health, safety, and welfare of the public. They represent a state's best effort to establish appropriate standards for a wide variety of professionals. To become a private practitioner in many of the rehabilitation services fields it is necessary to be licensed by, and abide by, the regulations of the appropriate state licensing board for that occupation.

In general, licensure requires that certain educational requirements have been met and that a certain number of hours of supervised clinical experience have been completed as part of the educational program of study. In many occupational fields, licensure also requires that a candidate have a specified number of years of experience working under the direct supervision of another licensed professional. Finally, licensure requires the passage of a written exam, and sometimes an oral exam.

While the doctorate is the highest level of educational attainment for a rehabilitation services professional, the licensed professional in any of these fields will have attained one of the highest levels of standing in that profession. Licensing of rehabilitation services professionals is a way for the public to know who has met the extensive and specific professional standards of the licensing board.

Licensing boards may revoke a person's license if there is just cause to do so. Just cause may include conviction of a felony or misdemeanor involving moral turpitude, gaining a license by fraud or misrepresentation, conducting a practice where the ability to practice safely is in question, negligence in professional conduct, or not conforming to the standards of practice for that profession.

WHAT IS CERTIFICATION?

Certification promotes professional responsibility, accountability, and visibility. It enables the public to identify those counselors who have met the professional standards set forth by the appropriate credentialing bodies.

Certification is intended to protect the public from those who are not qualified to provide a particular form of rehabilitation service. It also provides a referral network for the public.

Through the registry of certified rehabilitation services professionals, the public has access to counselors, therapists, and practitioners who have the professional accountability and recognition awarded to them by the appropriate certifying agency. The certification means that each professional in the registry has successfully fulfilled the educational and/or experiential requirements for certification.

The purpose of certification organizations is to provide the public with the assurance that professionals engaged in their particular practice of rehabilitation services have met the established standards of preparation at the time that they enter the profession. Periodic renewal of certification assures that these standards are maintained throughout the professional's career.

Certifying organizations establish and monitor certification systems appropriate to their particular fields. In addition, they identify and register those professionals who have voluntarily sought and gained certification.

Certification is generally awarded for a specific period of time. Completion of a specified number of hours of continuing professional education is required to renew the certification at the conclusion of this time. This assures that professionals are keeping up to date with changes in their field. The intent of any certification process is to provide a national standard of performance and professional behavior in the field.

WHO NEEDS CERTIFICATION AND LICENSURE?

Anyone who offers medical, therapeutic, and/or counseling services to the public needs either a license or certification, or both. In some occupations you must be licensed and certified before you can be employed in an agency or organization. In other occupations, licensure and certification are required only if you intend to enter private practice.

It is important to learn all you can about the requirements of your field of interest. It is also important that you stay informed because licensure and certification requirements can change over time. You always want to know what your occupational field demands.

WHO PROVIDES IT?

Depending on the occupational field, certification is usually provided by the appropriate professional organization or a subsidiary of that organization. Many professional associations have established separate certification boards to handle this aspect of their members' professional life.

Licensure of rehabilitation services professionals is done through state licensure boards or committees. These agencies license a wide variety of professionals. Each group has its own examining and licensure board. These boards are made up of licensed professionals in the field; they monitor the examination and licensure process and hear cases to revoke the license of a professional in the field.

THE IMPACT OF LEGISLATION AND TECHNOLOGY

Technology and legislation are two major areas that constantly impact rehabilitation services. Few other fields are as susceptible to changes in these areas.

Consider that employment opportunities are tied very closely to federal, state, and local funding. Changes in legislation can open and close opportunities in the field very quickly. Look on any professional association's website and you will find pages and links devoted to legislative issues of importance to that particular field. In addition, you will notice that most have located their headquarters in the Washington, D.C., area. They know how important legislative priorities and government funding can be to the careers of their members and to their patients and clients. They want to be close at hand to represent the interests of their members and the members' clients/patients.

Likewise technology and advances in science impact the treatment and care for patients/clients. With the technological explosion of the last 30 years, many rehabilitation services occupations have had to change their professional standards of care to keep pace. As researchers identify new techniques and new technologies for the rehabilitation of many disabling conditions, continuing education is becoming increasingly important.

LEGISLATIVE HISTORY AND ITS IMPACT ON REHABILITATION SERVICES

Over the past century a series of laws has been passed in Washington, D.C. Each piece of legislation defined the term *disability* and described how the federal government expected the states to serve those who were determined to be disabled. Each piece of legislation also funded specific activities in the area of rehabilitation services.

The initial legislation was aimed at the rehabilitation of war veterans. The scope of the original legislation was limited to rehabilitating veterans for entry into the workforce. The federal government gave funds to each state to take care of its own veterans through the state's vocational education board.

Today, organizations such as Disabled American Veterans (DAV) continue to monitor legislation concerned with veterans' benefits. Their staff of social and rehabilitation professionals also provide counseling, claims representation to veterans and their families, emergency relief for disabled veterans, and scholarships for children of needy disabled veterans. These staff members also advocate for local employment programs and removal of architectural and other barriers in the home and workplace.

Subsequent laws expanded not only the definition of *disabled* but also the populations that could be served. Later laws included nonveterans with severe physical and mental disabilities as well as mental retardation. The laws also broadened the scope of services beyond job placement. There was legislation that funded medical services, including surgery; counseling services for the disabled and their families; construction of facilities for persons with various types of disabilities; and education and training of a wide variety of rehabilitation services professionals.

Passage of the Americans with Disabilities Act (ADA) has continued the process of bringing disabled citizens into the mainstream of American life. By targeting employment, transportation, public service, and communications, this act has broadened the scope of services available to people with disabilities. It has also expanded the responsibilities of both rehabilitation services professionals and the business community in addressing the needs of the physically and mentally disabled.

The ADA has led to the development of organizations like Job Accommodation Network (JAN). JAN was sponsored by the President's Committee on Employment of People with Disabilities. It provides businesses with information and consultation on government policies and recommended worksite modifications. Rehabilitation experts are working not only with clients with disabilities but also with the organizations that employ them. The goal is to ensure that the workplace accommodates people with disabilities so that they can make a productive contribution to their employers and to society.

The National Rehabilitation Association was just one of many social and rehabilitation services associations that played an active role in the passage of ADA. Since its passage, these professionals have observed new opportunities for employment, socialization, and community participation created by ADA for people with disabilities. However, they feel that more needs to be done because of the continued high unemployment rate among people with disabilities. Therefore, they remain active in the legislative process.

On the international scene, Rehabilitation International is a federation of more than 100 organizations in 89 countries. Rehabilitation International lobbies for legislation on issues of disability prevention and rehabilitation worldwide, thus creating various opportunities for social and rehabilitation services professionals around the world.

The most recent federal initiative to impact the social and rehabilitation services field is legislation known as Welfare to Work (WtW). It has been unfolding over the past few years and is designed to help welfare recipients and other low-income Americans move into employment. WtW legislation is aimed at helping the hardest-to-employ recipients of welfare assistance to prepare for employment, find jobs, and stay employed. It has greatly increased the opportunities for social and rehabilitation services professionals to work in the areas of employment readiness and placement.

THE IMPACT OF TECHNOLOGY ON REHABILITATION SERVICES PROFESSIONALS AND THE PEOPLE THEY SERVE

The impact of technology on the rehabilitation services field is unlimited. Every day, advances in technology make the work of rehabilitation services professionals easier and improve the quality of life for their clients/patients.

Today, rehabilitation services administrators are able to computerize patient/client records, transmit reports to other members of the treatment team via electronic mail systems, and prepare agency payrolls. Employment services professionals are able to use computerized job searches and career-interest inventories with clients who previously were unable to access such assistance.

In the area of physical therapy, computer-based technology is being used to stimulate the muscles in the legs of paraplegic patients allowing them to walk and ride bicycles. Electronic sensors and computer-based systems are now available to allow a quadriplegic person to communicate through a computer. With further adaptation, it is expected that the system will even allow such patients to control the functions of a robotic arm by blinking their eyes.

Laser surgical techniques also hold new promise for many people with disabilities. Such surgeries as hip replacements have become almost commonplace as a result of advances in technology and robotic surgical equipment. This means that many elderly workers can increase the duration of their time in the workforce.

With the introduction of computer-aided design, work and living areas can now be planned and adapted for persons with disabilities. In fact, there is now an interdisciplinary group of rehabilitation engineers, occupational and physical therapists, and others in the rehabilitation field who are concerned with providing modern technology to persons with disabilities. The group is known as the Rehabilitation Engineering and Assistive Technology Society of North America (RESNA). In addition, the Electronics Industries Foundation (EIF) operates the Rehabilitation Engineering Center, which promotes commercial availability of assistive devices.

Unfortunately, there are very few rehabilitation services professionals who are as computer literate as they need to be. It will become increasingly important that the new professionals in this field become knowledgeable about the capabilities and limitations of technology as it applies to social and rehabilitation services areas. It will be their expertise in psychology, human development, anatomy, and recovery that will be vital to the full implementation of technology to the benefit of their patients/clients.

HOW TO READ THE TEA LEAVES

While technology and legislation may appear to be far removed from rehabilitation services, those who are considering a career in this area should be aware of just how these two phenomena can impact their career. It is important to keep up with current events not only on television but also on the Web, in magazines, and in newspapers.

Increased attention is being paid to the health-care delivery system in this country. How will the actions in Washington, D.C., and your state capital impact the occupational field in which you are interested? Will the recommended legislation limit or expand your earning potential? Will it provide more or fewer opportunities for you to pursue your education in your chosen field? How will it impact employment opportunities in that field?

It is also important to be knowledgeable about advances in technology that impact the occupations and the patients/clients in which you are interested. It is important to become more aware of the emerging technologies in your field. Use educational programs outside of school and/or elective courses in school. Having this knowledge can make you more competitive in a tough job market.

You may be thinking that you don't like computers and technology. After all, you are a people person. However, consider whether or not you will be able to be truly helpful to the people you decide to serve if you do not stay current about the capabilities of the new technologies.

Rehabilitation services careers offer challenge, responsibility, and reward to those who are well prepared and willing to work hard on behalf of the people they want to help.

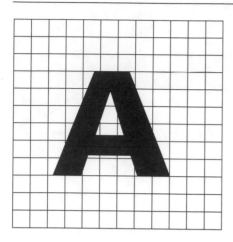

PROFESSIONAL ORGANIZATIONS

American Art Therapy Association, Inc.
1202 Allanson Road
Mundelein, Illinois 60060-3808
http://www.arttherapy.org/

American Counseling Association (ACA)
5999 Stevenson Avenue
Alexandria, VA 22304
http://www.counseling.org/

ACA Divisions with the Same Contact Information as Above:

American College Counseling Association (ACCA)
American Mental Health Counselors Association (AMHCA)
American Rehabilitation Counseling Association (ARCA)
American School Counselor Association (ASCA)
Association for Adult Development and Aging (AADA)
Association for Assessment in Counseling (AAC)
Association for Counselors and Educators in Government (ACEG)
Association for Counselor Education and Supervision (ACES)
Association for Gay, Lesbian and Bisexual Issues in Counseling
    (AGLBIC)
Association for Multicultural Counseling and Development (AMCD)
Association for Spiritual, Ethical, and Religious Values in Counseling
    (ASERVIC)
Association for Specialists in Group Work (ASGW)
Counseling Association for Humanistic Education and Development
    (C-AHEAD)
Counselors for Social Justice
International Association of Addiction and Offender Counselors (IAAOC)

International Association of Marriage and Family Counselors
    (IAMFC)
National Career Development Association (NCDA)
National Employment Counseling Association
    (NECA)

American Dance Therapy Association
2000 Century Plaza, Suite 108
10632 Little Patuxent Parkway
Columbia, MD 21044
http://www.adta.org

American Federation of State, County, and
    Municipal Employees
1625 L Street NW
Washington, DC 20036
http://www.afscme.org

American Geriatrics Society
Empire State Building
350 Fifth Avenue, Suite 801
New York, NY 10118
http://www.americangeriatrics.org

American Horticultural Therapy Association
909 York Street
Denver, CO 80206
http://www.ahta.org

American Music Therapy Association, Inc.
8455 Colesville Road, Suite 1000
Silver Spring, MD 20910
http://www.musictherapy.org

American Occupational Therapy Association
4720 Montgomery Lane
P.O. Box 31220
Bethesda, MD 20824-1220
http://www.aota.org

American Occupational Therapy Foundation
(A source of scholarship information)
4720 Montgomery Lane
P.O. Box 31220
Bethesda, MD 20824-1220
http://www.aota.org/featured/area2/index.asp

American Physical Therapy Association, Inc.
400 West 15th Street, Suite 805
Austin, TX 78701
http://www.apta.org

American Psychiatric Association
1400 K Street NW
Washington, DC 20005
http://www.psych.org

American Psychological Association (APA)
750 First Street NE, Suite 100
Washington, DC 20002
http://www.apa.org

*APA Divisions with the Same Contact Information as Above
(APA Division Numbers Follow):*

Addictions (50)
Adult Development and Aging (20)
American Psychology-Law Society (41)
Applied Experimental and Engineering Psychology (21)
Behavioral Neuroscience and Comparative Psychology (6)
Child, Youth, and Family Services (37)
Clinical Child Psychology (Division 12, Section 1)
Clinical Neuropsychology (40)
Consulting Psychology (13)
Counseling Psychology (17)
Developmental Psychology (7)
Educational Psychology (15)
Evaluation, Measurement, and Statistics (5)
Exercise and Sport Psychology (47)
Experimental Analysis of Behavior (25)
Experimental Psychology (3)
Family Psychology (43)
Group Psychology and Group Psychotherapy (49)
Health Psychology (38)
History of Psychology (26)
Humanistic Psychology (32)
International Psychology (52)
Media Psychology (46)
Mental Retardation and Developmental
   Disabilities (33)
Military Psychology (19)
Peace Psychology (48)
Population and Environmental Psychology (34)
Psychoanalysis (39)

Psychological Hypnosis (30)
Psychologists in Independent Practice (42)
Psychologists in Public Service (18)
Psychology and the Arts (10)
Psychology of Religion (36)
Psychopharmacology and Substance Abuse (28)
Psychotherapy (29)
Rehabilitation Psychology (22)
School Psychology (16)
Society of Clinical Psychology (12)
Society for Community Research and Action: Division of Community
   Psychology (27)
Society for Consumer Psychology (23)
Society for General Psychology (1)
Society for Industrial and Organizational Psychology (14)
Society of Pediatric Psychology (Division 12, Section V) (54)
Society of Personality and Social Psychology (8)
Society for the Psychological Study of Ethnic Minority Issues (45)
Society for the Psychological Study of Lesbian and Gay Issues (44)
Society for the Psychological Study of Men and Masculinity (51)
Society for the Psychological Study of Social Issues (9)
Society for the Psychology of Women (35)
Society for the Teaching of Psychology (2)
State Psychological Association Affairs (31)
Theoretical and Philosophical Psychology (24)

American Rehabilitation Counseling Association
5999 Stevenson Avenue
Alexandria, VA 22304
http://www.nchrtm.okstate.edu/arca

American School Counselor Association
5999 Stevenson Avenue
Alexandria, VA 22304
http://www.schoolcounselor.org

American Therapeutic Recreation Association
1414 Prince Street, Suite 204
Alexandria, VA 22314
http://www.atra-tr.org

Association for Career and Technical Education
(Formerly American Vocational Association)
1410 King Street
Alexandria, VA 22314
http://www.acteonline.org

Association for Play Therapy, Inc.
2050 North Winery Avenue, Suite 101
Fresno, CA 93703
http://www.iapt.org

Council on Rehabilitation Education
1835 Rohlwing Road, Suite E
Rolling Meadows, IL 60008
http://www.core-rehab.org

Council on Social Work Education
1725 Duke Street, Suite 500
Alexandria, VA 22314
(Publishes the *Directory of Accredited B.S.W. and M.S.W. Programs*)
http://www.cswe.org

Hebrew Union College
Jewish Institute of Religion
One West Fourth Street
New York, NY 10012

Jewish Theological Seminary of America
3080 Broadway
New York, NY 10027
http://www.jtsa.edu

National Association of Colleges and Employers
(Formerly College Placement Council)
62 Highland Avenue
Bethlehem, PA 18017-9085
http://www.naceweb.org

National Association of Rehabilitation Facilities in the Private Sector
P.O. Box 697
Brookline, MA 02146
http://www.arcat.com

National Association of School Psychologists
4340 East West Highway, Suite 402
Bethesda, MD 20814
http://www.naspweb.org

National Association of Social Workers (NASW)
750 First Street NE, Suite 700
Washington, DC 20002-4241
http://www.naswdc.org

For the NASW section on Alcohol, Tobacco and Other Drugs (ATOD); Private Practice (PP); and Aging, see http://www.naswdc.org/sections.

National Clearinghouse on Alcoholism and Drug Abuse Information
P.O. Box 2345
Rockville, MD 20852
http://www.health.org

National Coalition for Church Vocations
5420 South Cornell Avenue #105
Chicago, IL 60615-5604
http://www.nccv-vocations.org

National Council on Disability
1331 F Street NW, Suite 1050
Washington, DC 20004-1107
http://www.ncd.gov

National Council on Rehabilitation Education
Department of Special Education and Rehabilitation
College of Education, Room 412
P.O. Box 210069
Tucson, AZ 85721
Website maintained at http://www.nchrtm.okstate.edu/ncre/ncre.html

National Employment Counseling Association
(A division of ACA)
5999 Stevenson Avenue
Alexandria, VA 22304
Website maintained at http://www.geocities.com/Athens/Acropolis/
    6491/neca.html

National Institute on Drug Abuse
6001 Executive Boulevard
Bethesda, MD 20892-9561
http://www.nida.nih.gov

National Rehabilitation Association
633 South Washington Street
Alexandria, VA 22314
http://www.nationalrehab.org

National Rehabilitation Counseling Association
8807 Sudley Road, Suite 102
Manassas, VA 22110-4719
http://www.nrca-net.org

National Therapeutic Recreation Society
22377 Belmont Ridge Road
Ashburn, VA 20148
http://www.nrpa.org/branches/ntrs.htm

People-Plant Council
Department of Horticulture (0327)
Virginia Polytechnic Institute and State University
Blacksburg, VA 24061
http://www.hort.vt.edu/human/ppcmenu.html

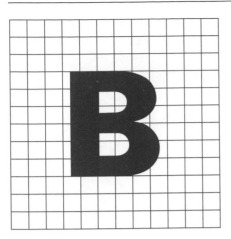

LICENSURE AND CERTIFICATION ORGANIZATIONS

American Academy of Orthotists and Prosthetists
1650 King Street, Suite 500
Alexandria, VA 22314
http://www.oandp.org

American Association of Psychotherapists, Inc.
P.O. Box 140182
Dallas, TX 75214
http://www.angelfire.com/tx/membership

American Association of State Social Work Boards
400 South Ridge Parkway, Suite B
Culpepper, VA 22701
(Contact for a list of regulatory agencies or for a comparison of state
    regulations)
http://www.aasswb.org

American Board of Examiners in Clinical Social Work
Shetland Park
27 Congress Street
Salem, MA 01970
http://www.abecsw.org

American Board of Professional Psychology
2100 East Broadway, Suite 313
Columbia, MO 65201-6082
http://www.abpp.org

American Board of Rehabilitation Psychology
750 First Street NE, Suite 100
Washington, DC 20002
http://www.apa.org/divisions/div22/ABRP.html

American Dietetic Association
216 West Jackson Boulevard, Suite 800
Chicago, IL 60606-6995
(312) 899-0040
http://www.eatright.org

American Horticultural Therapy Association
909 York Street
Denver, CO 80206
http://www.ahta.org

American Medical Association
535 North Dearborn Street
Chicago, IL 60610
http://www.ama-assn.org

American Music Therapy Association, Inc.
8455 Colesville Road, Suite 1000
Silver Spring, MD 20910
http://www.musictherapy.org

American Occupational Therapy Certification Board
4720 Montgomery Lane
P.O. Box 31220
Bethesda, MD 20824-1220
http://www.aota.org

American Physical Therapy Association
400 West 15th Street, Suite 805
Austin, TX 78701
http://www.apta.org

American Psychological Association
750 First Street NE, Suite 100
Washington, DC 20002
http://www.apa.org

American Speech-Language-Hearing Certification
10801 Rockville Pike
Rockville, MD 20852
http://www.asha.org

Art Therapy Credentials Board, Inc.
3 Terrace Way, Suite B
Greensboro, NC 27403
http://www.atcb.org

Association of State and Provincial
    Psychology Boards
P.O. Box 241245
Mongtomery, AL 36124-1245
http://www.asppb.org

Center for Credentialing & Education, Inc. (CCE)
3 Terrace Way, Suite D
Greensboro, NC 27403
http://www.cce-global.org

Commission on Rehabilitation Counselor Education
1835 Rohlwing Road, Suite E
Rolling Meadows, IL 60008
http://www.core-rehab.org

Council for Accreditation of Counseling and Related
    Educational Programs
5999 Stevenson Avenue, 4th Floor
Alexandria, VA 22304
http://www.counseling.org/cacrep

Council for Higher Education Accreditation
One Dupont Circle NW, Suite 510
Washington, DC 20036-1135
http://www.chea.org

Council on Rehabilitation Education
1835 Rohlwing Road, Suite E
Rolling Meadows, IL 60008
http://www.core-rehab.org

National Academy of Certified Clinical Mental
    Health Counselors
5999 Stevenson Avenue
Alexandria, VA 22304

National Board for Certified Counselors
3 Terrace Way, Suite D
Greensboro, NC 27403
http://www.nbcc.org

National Commission on Orthotic and Prosthetic Education
1650 King Street, Suite 500
Alexandria, VA 22314
http://www.ncope.org

National Council for Therapeutic Recreation Certification
7 Elmwood Drive
New City, NY 10956
http://www.nctrc.org

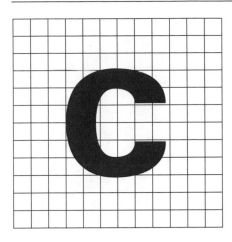

ADDITIONAL ORGANIZATIONS

Academy of Counseling Psychology
http://hometown.net/academy/academy.htm

American Association for Geriatric Psychiatry
http://www.aagpgpa.org

American Association for Marriage and Family Therapy
http://www.aamft.org

American Association for Psychology and the Performing Arts
http://members.tripod.com

American Association of Pastoral Counselors
http://www.aapc.org

American Association of State Social Work Boards
http://www.aasswb.org

American Board of Examiners in Clinical Social Work
http://www.abecsw.org

American Board of Professional Psychology
http://www.abpp.org

American Medical Association
http://www.ama-assn.org

American Mental Health Counselors Association (AMHCA)
http://www.amhca.org/home2.html

American Psychiatric Association
http://www.psych.org

American Psychiatric Nurses Association
http://www.apna.org

American Psychoanalytic Association
http://apsa.org

American Psychological Society
http://www.psychologicalscience.org

Asian American Psychological Association
http://www.west.asu.edu/aapa

Association for the Advancement of Psychology
http://www.aapnet.org/

Association for Death Education and Counseling
http://www.adec.org

Association of Black Psychologists
http://www.abpsi.org

Association of Occupational Therapists in Mental Health
http://www.iop.bpmf.ac.uk/home/trust/ot/aotmh.htm

Association for Specialists in Group Work
http://blues.fd1.uc.edu/~wilson/asgw

Clinical Social Work Federation
http://www.cswf.org

Institute of Gerontology, Wayne State University
http://www.iog.wayne.edu

International Association of Applied Psychology
http://www.ucm.es/info/Psyap/iaap

International Association of Cognitive Psychotherapy
http://www.personal.kent.edu/~iacp

International Association of Marriage and Family Counselors
http://www.iamfc.org

International Association of Psychosocial Rehabilitation Services
http://www.iapsrs.org

International Association of Spiritual Psychiatry
http://essence-euro.org/iasp

International Federation of Social Workers
http://www.ifsw.org

National Association of Alcoholism & Drug Abuse Counselors
http://www.naadac.org

National Association of School Psychologists
http://www.naspweb.org

National Institute on Alcohol Abuse and Alcoholism
http://www.niaaa.nih.gov

Society for Computers in Psychology, Lafayette College
http://www.lafayette.edu/allanr/scip.html

Society for Industrial and Organizational Psychology
http://www.siop.org

Society for Personality and Social Psychology
http://www.spsp.org/

Society for Police and Criminal Psychology
http://www.jmu.edu/psyc/spcp

World Council for Psychotherapy
http://www.ping.at/social-development/wcp

World Health Organization
http://www.who.ch

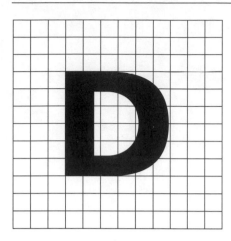

UNIVERSITIES AND COLLEGES

Following is a sampling of the many universities and colleges that offer graduate and undergraduate programs in social and rehabilitation services. Check out these websites for more information about individual schools and programs.

Universities and Colleges with Social Work Programs

Adelphi University (NY)
http://www.adelphi.edu

Andrews University (MI)
http://www.andrews.edu

Arizona State University
http://www.asu.edu

Ashland University (OH)
http://www.ashland.edu

Austin Peay State University (TN)
http://www.apsu.edu

Ball State University (IN)
http://www.bsu.edu

Barry University (FL)
http://www.barry.edu

Baylor University (TX)
http://www.baylor.edu

Bloomsburg University (PA)
http://www.bloomu.edu

Boston College
http://www.bc.edu

Boston University
http://www.bu.edu

Brigham Young University (UT)
http://www.byu.edu

Bryn Mawr College (PA)
http://www.brynmawr.edu

Central Michigan University
http://www.cmich.edu

Clark Atlanta University (GA)
http://www.cau.edu

Columbia University (NY)
http://www.columbia.edu

Delta State University (MS)
http://www.deltast.edu

Eastern Washington University (WA)
http://www.ewu.edu

Ferrum College (VA)
http://www.ferrum.edu/indexjava.htm

Florida International University
http://www.fiu.edu/choice.html

Gallaudet University (DC)
http://www.gallaudet.edu

Hood College (MD)
http://www.hood.edu

Hope College (MI)
http://www.hope.edu

Hunter College (NY)
http://www.hunter.cuny.edu

Idaho State University
http://www.isu.edu

Indiana University
http://www.indiana.edu

James Madison University (VA)
http://www.jmu.edu

Kansas State University
http://www.ksu.edu

Kean University (NJ)
http://www.kean.edu

Loma Linda University (CA)
http://www.llu.edu

Loyola University Chicago
http://www.luc.edu

Marian College (WI)
http://www.mariancoll.edu

Monmouth University (NJ)
http://www.monmouth.edu

Nebraska Wesleyan University
http://www.nebrwesleyan.edu

New Mexico State University
http://www.nmsu.edu

North Carolina State University
http://www.ncsu.edu

Northern Arizona University
http://www.nau.edu

Oakwood College (AL)
http://www.oakwood.edu

Oklahoma Baptist University
http://www.okbu.edu

Pacific Lutheran University (WA)
http://www.plu.edu

Saginaw Valley State University (MI)
http://www.svsu.edu

Shippensburg University (PA)
http://www.ship.edu

Temple University (PA)
http://www.temple.edu

Texas Woman's University
http://www.twu.edu

Trevecca Nazarene University (TN)
http://www.trevecca.edu

Tulane University (LA)
www2.tulane.edu

University of Alaska at Anchorage
http://www.uaa.alaska.edu/socwork

University of Chicago
http://www.uchicago.edu

University of Cincinnati
http://www.uc.edu

University of Denver
http://www.du.edu

University of Minnesota
http://www.umn.edu

University of Montana
http://www.umt.edu

Walla Walla College (WA)
http://www.wwc.edu/nav

Washington University (MO)
http://www.wustl.edu

Xavier University (OH)
http://www.xu.edu

Yeshiva University (NY)
http://www.yu.edu

Universities and Colleges with Rehabilitation Counseling Programs

Alabama A&M University
http://www.aamu.edu

Arkansas State University
http://www.asumh.edu

Assumption College (MA)
http://www.assumption.edu

Bowling Green State University
   (OH)
http://www.bgsu.edu

Coppin State College (MD)
http://www.coppin.edu

Drake University (IA)
http://www.drake.edu

East Central University (OK)
http://www.ecok.edu

Edinboro University of Pennsylvania
http://www.edinboro.edu

Fort Valley State University (GA)
http://www.fvsu.edu

George Washington University (DC)
http://www.gwu.edu

Georgia State University
http://www.gsu.edu

Hofstra University (NY)
http://www.hofstra.edu

Illinois Institute of Technology
http://www.iit.edu

Kent State University (OH)
http://www.kent.edu

Mississippi State University
http://www.msstate.edu

Montana State University at Billings
http://www.msubillings.edu

Northeastern University (MA)
http://www.northeastern.edu

Pennsylvania State University
http://www.psu.edu

San Francisco State University
   (CA)
http://www.sfsu.edu

South Carolina State University
http://www.scsu.edu

Springfield College
(MA)
http://www.spfldcol.edu

Stephen F. Austin State University
(TX)
http://www.sfasu.edu

University of Arizona
http://www.arizona.edu

University of Florida
http://www.ufl.edu

University of Idaho
http://www.uidaho.edu

University of Iowa
http://www.uiowa.edu

University of Massachusetts at
Boston
http://www.umb.edu

University of Memphis (TN)
http://www.memphis.edu

University of Northern Colorado
http://www.univnorthco.edu

University of Puerto Rico
http://www.upr.clu.edu

University of Scranton (PA)
http://www.scranton.edu

University of Southern Maine
http://www.usm.maine.edu

University of Texas at Austin
http://www.utexas.edu

Western Oregon University
http://www.wou.edu

Wright State University (OH)
http://www.wright.edu

Universities and Colleges with Programs in Both Fields

Auburn University (AL)
http://www.auburn.edu

California State University
at Fresno
http://www.csifresno.edu

California State University at
Sacramento
http://www.csus.edu

California State University at
San Bernardino
http://www.csusb.edu

Florida State University
http://www.fsu.edu

Jackson State University
(MS)
http://www.jsums.edu

Louisiana State University
http://www.lsu.edu/index2.html

Minnesota State University at
Mankato
http://www.mankato.msus.edu

Michigan State University
http://www.msu.edu

New York University
http://www.nyu.edu

Ohio State University
http://www.osu.edu

Portland State University (OR)
http://www.pdx.edu

San Diego State University (CA)
http://www.sdsu.edu

St. Cloud State University (MN)
http://www.stcloudstate.edu

Syracuse University (NY)
http://www.syr.edu

University of Arkansas at Little
   Rock
http://www.ualr.edu

University of Georgia
http://www.uga.edu

University of Hawaii at Manoa
http://www.uhm.hawaii.edu

University of Illinois at Urbana-
   Champaign
http://www.uiuc.edu

University of Kentucky
http://www.uky.edu

University of Maryland at Baltimore
   County
http://www.umbc.edu

University of Missouri
http://www.system.missouri.edu

University of North Carolina at
   Chapel Hill
http://www.unc.edu

University of Tennessee at
   Knoxville
http://www.utk.edu

Utah State University
http://www.usu.edu

Virginia Commonwealth University
http://www.vcu.edu

Wayne State University (MI)
http://www.wayne.edu

West Virginia University
http://www.wvu.edu

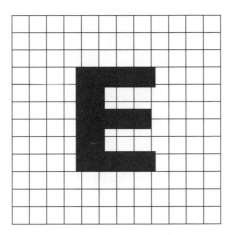

RECOMMENDED READING

Burger, William. *The Helping Professions: A Careers Sourcebook.* Wadsworth Publishing Company, 1999.

Collison, Brooke, and Nancy Garfield. *Careers in Counseling and Human Services.* Taylor & Francis, 1996.

Colvin, Donna, and Ralph Nader. *Good Works: A Guide to Careers in Social Change.* Barricade Books, 1994.

DeGalan, Julie, and Stephen Lambert. *Great Jobs for Psychology Majors, Second Edition.* VGM Career Books, 2000.

Doelling, Carol. *Social Work Career Development: A Handbook for Job Hunting and Career Planning.* National Association of Social Workers, 1997.

The Editors of VGM Career Books. *Resumes for Social Service Careers.* VGM Career Books, 2000.

Everett, Melissa. *Making a Living While Making a Difference.* New Society Publishers, 1999.

Gran, Gary, and Linda Grobman. *The Social Worker's Internet Handbook.* White Hat Communications, 1998.

Sternberg, Robert. *Career Paths in Psychology: Where Your Degree Can Take You.* American Psychological Association, 1997.

Super, Charles, and Donald Super. *Opportunities in Psychology Careers.* VGM Career Books, 2001.

Wittenberg, Renee. *Opportunities in Social Work Careers.* VGM Career Books, 1997.